AI-Powered
Decision Making

by
Shawn Carter

AI-Powered Decision Making

Contents

Introduction

In today's rapidly evolving business landscape, the infusion of Artificial Intelligence (AI) into strategic decision-making is not just a competitive edge—it's becoming a necessity. The world is witnessing an unprecedented transformation, where data-driven decisions powered by AI forge new paths in efficiency and innovation. Business leaders and professionals find themselves at the cusp of a technological revolution that promises to redefine the norms of enterprise operations.

For many, AI might seem like a distant concept relegated to tech-savvy organizations or Silicon Valley gurus. However, its real power lies in its accessibility and adaptability across various sectors. AI is no longer confined to theoretical discussions or laboratory experiments; it's a tangible force impacting everything from marketing strategies to supply chain logistics. The time has come for industries of all stripes to harness this potential, transforming challenges into opportunities with the right knowledge and tools.

Imagine automating routine processes, anticipating market trends through predictive analytics, or personalizing customer experiences to an unprecedented degree. Such applications of AI can unlock new potential and revenues, putting businesses ahead in today's competitive markets. As we embark on this journey, it becomes imperative to grasp the foundational concepts and understand how to effectively integrate AI into everyday decision-making.

The objective of this book is straightforward: to equip you, a business leader or professional, with the insights and strategies required to employ AI effectively within your organization. Whether you are a seasoned manager, an aspiring leader, or someone eager to innovate through technology, this guide will serve as a roadmap to seamlessly incorporate AI into your business processes.

We'll explore how modern enterprises can leverage AI for strategic advantage, identifying the benefits that AI-driven strategies provide. It involves understanding key concepts such as machine learning, predictive analytics, and data management—collectively forming the bedrock of AI integration. Rather than focusing on the minutiae of technical jargon, our aim is to demystify these elements and present them in a way that is both approachable and actionable, providing insights that are relatable and applicable to real-world business scenarios.

In the subsequent chapters, we will dive deeper into AI's role in various business functions—right from marketing to human resources, finance, and operations. The vast array of potential applications makes AI a versatile tool, adaptable to diverse needs and unique business landscapes. By aligning AI strategies with business goals, organizations can cultivate a symbiotic relationship where technology acts not as a substitute but as an enhancer of human initiative and creativity.

Equally critical is addressing the ethical considerations that come hand-in-hand with AI adoption. Ensuring transparency, accountability, and fairness within AI systems will be pivotal in building trust and safeguarding interests. As the deployment of AI tools expands, navigating the complex regulatory and legal landscapes will also be integral to organizational success.

One of the greatest challenges lies in the implementation and scaling of AI initiatives. Organizations may face hurdles ranging from technological bottlenecks to cultural resistance. Here, we offer

strategies for overcoming such barriers, emphasizing the importance of an adaptable mindset and fostering a culture that embraces data-driven decision-making as a cornerstone of business operations.

Finally, we aim to inspire. By examining real-world case studies of successful AI applications across industries, readers can draw lessons from those who have blazed the trail before them. These stories of innovation serve as both motivation and validation, illustrating AI's transformative potential when used effectively and responsibly.

The future holds immense possibilities, with emerging AI technologies poised to further change the landscape. Whether it's deploying advanced machine learning models, assessing AI's impact through well-defined KPIs, or simply staying abreast of burgeoning trends, anticipating what's to come is as crucial as understanding the current capabilities.

As we begin this exciting exploration, prepare to not only embrace AI as a tool but as a partner in crafting strategies for achieving tomorrow's competitive advantage today. Welcome to the world of AI in business, where the only limits are the bounds of your imagination and the extent of your ambition.

Chapter 1:
Understanding AI in Business

In the fast-paced world of modern enterprise, grasping the potential of Artificial Intelligence is no longer optional—it's essential. As companies strive to remain competitive, AI emerges as a pivotal tool for redefining business strategies and enhancing decision-making processes. By automating routine tasks and generating insights from vast swathes of data, AI not only streamlines operations but also unveils new opportunities for innovation and growth. Visionary business leaders are finding that integrating AI into their core functions can lead to improved efficiency and a significant competitive edge. As we unravel this transformative technology, it's crucial to understand its role in shaping contemporary enterprises and paving the way for groundbreaking advancements. AI-driven strategies aren't just about keeping pace; they're about setting the pace for the future, inviting businesses to leverage its power for sustainable success and industry leadership.

The Role of AI in Modern Enterprises

Artificial Intelligence (AI) has revolutionized how modern enterprises operate, redefining strategies across industries. The once cutting-edge technology has now become a crucial component for business leaders looking to gain a competitive edge. Whether it's for streamlining operations, enhancing customer experiences, or driving innovations,

AI's potential seems limitless. But what does the role of AI truly entail in the context of today's enterprises?

In the modern enterprise landscape, AI is more than a mere tool — it's a strategic partner. Companies that have successfully integrated AI into their core operations often view it as an indispensable ally in decision-making processes. This symbiotic relationship empowers businesses to make data-driven decisions at unprecedented scales and speeds. The ability to analyze vast amounts of data quickly allows enterprises to identify trends, understand customer behaviors, and predict market shifts that keep them ahead of the curve.

AI technologies also contribute significantly to increased operational efficiency. By automating routine tasks, enterprises free up human resources for more complex, creative, and strategic initiatives. For instance, chatbots and virtual assistants handle customer inquiries around-the-clock, reducing the burden on human support teams while providing faster response times to customer queries. Such automation not only streamlines processes but also positions companies to offer consistently high levels of service.

One cannot overlook AI's critical role in facilitating innovation. Through machine learning and predictive analytics, enterprises can venture into new markets with more confidence. AI enables businesses to experiment with different models and scenarios without undergoing the cost and risk of actual execution. This fosters an environment where innovation thrives, encouraging enterprises to push boundaries and redefine industries.

AI's influence extends to strategic marketing as well. By analyzing consumer data, AI provides invaluable insights into customer preferences and purchasing habits. This data helps enterprises tailor their marketing strategies to target specific segments more effectively. Personalized marketing campaigns that resonate with individual customers lead to increased engagement and conversion rates, giving companies a substantial advantage over their competitors.

Moreover, AI's integration into supply chain management has redefined logistical capabilities. Predictive analytics facilitate demand forecasting, allowing enterprises to maintain optimal inventory levels and minimize wastage. AI-driven analytics can identify potential supply chain disruptions and recommend proactive measures, ensuring smooth operations even in unpredictable circumstances. The seamless integration of AI in logistics maximizes resource utilization and reduces operational costs.

AI plays an essential role in enhancing financial decision-making processes as well. Advanced algorithms capable of identifying patterns in large datasets equip financial managers with tools to assess risks and optimize investment portfolios. Such insights support informed decision-making, improving financial outcomes and driving stronger business growth. For enterprises, gaining true visibility and insight into market dynamics creates opportunities to capitalize on emerging trends ahead of competitors.

While AI's potential is indeed transformative, businesses must tread carefully to harness its capabilities responsibly. Issues such as data privacy, ethics, and bias remain critical considerations. Enterprises that champion transparent and ethical AI practices not only gain trust from customers but also pave the way for sustainable success.

Successful integration of AI into business models requires a coherent strategy that's aligned with the company's overarching goals. Enterprises need to assess their unique challenges and define core areas where AI can deliver the greatest impact. Collaborating with AI experts and fostering AI skills within teams will also ensure that businesses can fully capitalize on AI's capabilities.

As businesses continue to adopt AI technologies, the role of AI will undoubtedly expand. It will continue to shape industries, drive economic growth, and transform how enterprises function in profound ways. Currently, AI holds the promise of innovation, efficiency, and competitiveness, offering modern enterprises opportunities to evolve in an ever-changing landscape.

Benefits of AI-Driven Strategies

In the dynamic landscape of modern business, integrating Artificial Intelligence (AI) into strategic frameworks has emerged as a transformative power. AI-driven strategies offer a unique blend of technological acumen and operational dexterity that can revolutionize business processes. By embedding AI in decision-making, companies harness the capacity to analyze massive datasets, predict outcomes, and implement solutions that were once beyond reach. The essence lies not just in the adoption of AI but in utilizing it to craft strategies that foster innovation, enhance productivity, and secure competitive advantage.

One of the most prominent benefits of AI-driven strategies is the increased operational efficiency they deliver. Businesses can automate repetitive and mundane tasks, allowing employees to engage in more complex and creative work. For instance, AI can manage inventory and supply chain logistics with precision, reducing human error and enhancing speed. In retail, AI's power to effectively manage inventory levels ensures resources are optimally allocated, minimizing waste and maximizing profit margins. This kind of efficiency boost is invaluable, especially in industries where margins are thin, and the speed of product turnovers is critical.

Moreover, AI enables companies to harness predictive analytics, a capability that can dramatically shift how businesses forecast market trends and consumer behavior. Predictive insights derived from AI models allow companies to anticipate changes in customer preferences or predict supply chain disruptions before they occur. This foresight equips businesses with the agility to respond proactively rather than reactively, giving them a strategic edge in rapidly changing environments. By predicting demand fluctuations, businesses can adjust their strategies to maximize sales and minimize losses.

Another significant advantage of AI-driven strategies is personalized customer engagement. AI technologies can analyze customer data to offer tailored recommendations and experiences. This personalization leads to greater customer satisfaction and loyalty, as consumers increasingly expect businesses to understand and anticipate their needs. In sectors such as e-commerce, hyper-personalization not only boosts customer experience but also significantly increases conversion rates, nurturing deeper customer relationships and driving business growth.

Decision-making processes within organizations also stand to gain from AI's prowess. AI systems can compile and analyze data from multiple sources, providing a coherent snapshot that enhances decision-making accuracy. Business leaders can rely on AI to sift through complex datasets and highlight patterns or anomalies that humans might overlook. This data-driven decision-making ensures that strategic choices are based on solid evidence, reducing the risk of costly missteps and allowing leaders to allocate resources more effectively.

AI-driven strategies enhance innovation by providing the tools to experiment with new ideas and models rapidly. Through AI, businesses can simulate environments to test strategies without the financial risks associated with trial-and-error methods in real-world scenarios. AI's ability to process diverse variables in these simulations means companies can innovate with confidence, exploring avenues such as new product development and market entry strategies from informed standpoints.

Furthermore, AI facilitates the development of robust risk management frameworks. By identifying potential risks early, AI systems allow companies to devise contingencies and mitigate risks before they escalate. This predictive capability is critical in sectors like finance and healthcare, where risk management is paramount. AI can alert businesses to financial anomalies or patient trends, enabling timely interventions that safeguard business continuity and enhance reputational value.

However, the benefits of AI-driven strategies extend beyond individual enterprises; they contribute to industry-wide advancements that redefine sectors. As more businesses adopt AI, a network effect emerges where shared learnings and improvements drive collective progress. Within industries, the adoption of AI can lead to standardization and the setting of best practices that elevate entire ecosystems, promoting innovation and competition.

Additionally, AI-driven strategies offer environmental benefits by enabling sustainable business practices. AI systems improve energy efficiency and reduce resource consumption, aiding businesses in meeting sustainability targets. For example, AI can optimize process workflows in manufacturing to minimize waste, or manage energy consumption in real-time, leading to notable reductions in carbon footprints. This not only bolsters a company's reputation but also aligns with the growing consumer demand for eco-friendly practices.

In the financial domain, AI strategies enhance investment portfolios through sophisticated analysis of financial data, leading to more informed and risk-adjusted investment decisions. AI can continuously scan market conditions, detect trends, and suggest strategic adjustments to portfolios that traditional analysis might miss.

Asset management firms leveraging AI see improved returns and client satisfaction, accentuating the advantages of AI integration.

In terms of workforce dynamics, AI-driven strategies foster a collaborative human-AI ecosystem. Rather than replacing jobs, AI augments human capabilities, leading to enhanced productivity and job satisfaction. By handling routine tasks, AI frees up human resources to focus on innovative and strategic tasks, fostering a more engaged and motivated workforce. This shift demands upskilling and reskilling initiatives, preparing employees to thrive alongside AI technologies.

AI-driven strategies are not just about technology; they're about transforming organizational mindsets and cultures to embrace data-driven insights. The cultural shift involves leadership buy-in and a commitment to ongoing learning and adaptation. By nurturing a data-driven culture, companies can ensure that their workforce is aligned with evolving strategic goals, fostering resilience and adaptability in the face of disruption.

Lastly, businesses employing AI-driven strategies can lead market disruption, continuously redefining industry standards and challenging competitors to innovate. Companies that swiftly adapt to AI's capabilities are better positioned to set trends rather than follow them, securing a foothold as industry leaders. This market positioning is essential in maintaining a long-term competitive advantage, particularly in industries undergoing rapid digital transformation.

In summary, the benefits of AI-driven strategies are multifaceted, offering both tangible and intangible advantages that empower businesses to thrive in a digital world. From enhancing operational efficiency and personalized customer engagement to driving innovation and managing risks, AI provides the tools and capabilities necessary for businesses to not only survive but also excel amidst competition. Embracing AI is not an option but a strategic imperative for businesses aiming to lead in the age of intelligent technology.

Chapter 2:
Foundations of AI-Powered Decision Making

Venturing into the intricate world of AI-powered decision-making demands a robust understanding of the foundational principles that drive this transformative technology. As businesses increasingly rely on artificial intelligence to sculpt strategic pathways, grasping the core concepts is crucial for maximizing potential and steering clear of common pitfalls. At its essence, AI empowers organizations to sift through vast silos of data, extracting actionable insights with unprecedented speed and precision. This capability not only enhances decision-making by spotlighting trends and predicting outcomes but also brings a level of agility that's vital in today's fast-paced market landscape. Data, often heralded as the new oil, functions as the lifeblood of AI, necessitating rigorous collection, storage, and refinement processes to unleash the full might of machine intelligence. Drawing from comprehensive datasets, AI redefines how enterprises perceive challenges, enabling leaders to pivot strategies based on real-time analytics. Embracing these foundational elements not only drives innovation but positions any enterprise to harness AI as a catalyst for sustainable growth and competitive edge.

Key Concepts in AI

In the landscape of AI-powered decision-making, understanding the key concepts of Artificial Intelligence is akin to mastering the rules of a strategic game. These concepts serve as the bedrock upon which complex systems and applications are built. At its core, AI involves the creation of systems that can perform tasks by mimicking human intelligence. But a mere definition falls short of capturing the myriad facets encompassed within AI.

One foundational concept is **machine learning**. This aspect of AI is not merely a tool, but a dynamic process that allows systems to improve over time. Unlike traditional programming where outputs are determined explicitly by coding, machine learning leverages data to derive its own rules. It's akin to teaching a machine through experience rather than instruction. By analyzing patterns and inferring insights from vast datasets, businesses can predict trends, recognize opportunities, and make informed decisions with a level of efficiency once thought impossible.

Neural networks form another critical pillar in AI, inspired by the human brain's network of neurons. These networks excel in identifying intricate patterns through layers of interconnected 'neurons', making them particularly potent for tasks such as image and speech recognition. Their capability to perform nonlinear transformations allows businesses to solve complex problems that traditional algorithms fail to tackle.

A closely related concept is **deep learning**, a subset of machine learning where neural networks with multiple layers are utilized to delve deeper into data. This depth enables AI systems to learn higher-level abstractions, a trait that has catalyzed breakthroughs in areas such as autonomous vehicles and medical imaging. For business leaders, embracing deep learning translates to tapping into a reservoir of advanced analytical capabilities.

Yet, AI is not just about learning and modeling. **Natural language processing (NLP)** provides systems the ability to understand and respond to human language. This opens the door to more intuitive human-computer interactions, from chatbots offering customer support to tools that analyze sentiment across social media. For businesses, NLP offers a means to bridge communication gaps and enhance user engagement.

Another indispensable concept is **automation**. AI-driven automation is revolutionizing industries by decreasing mundane tasks and augmenting human capabilities. Automation extends beyond rudimentary tasks; it encompasses the entire lifecycle of a decision-making process—from data preparation to execution. The integration of AI-driven automation helps businesses reallocate human resources towards strategic, high-impact activities.

Robotics also plays a vital role in the realm of AI, transforming industries by automating physical tasks. From manufacturing floors to warehouses, AI-enhanced robots adapt to new conditions, reducing errors and improving productivity. They collaborate, rather than replace, human workers, thus fostering an environment where technology and labor harmoniously coexist.

Data mining underpins much of what AI accomplishes. This process, involving the extraction of actionable insights from vast amounts of data, is crucial in driving decisions based on patterns and trends that might otherwise remain hidden. For leaders, the ability to derive value from data ensures businesses stay ahead of the curve in an increasingly data-centric world.

The essence of AI and its key concepts culminate in the creation of a **smart ecosystem**. Here, AI integrates seamlessly with day-to-day business operations, enabling adaptive and intelligent workflows. Imagine systems that dynamically adjust marketing campaigns or supply chains that predict and mitigate disruptions before they occur.

This intelligent interconnectivity empowers organizations to achieve unparalleled levels of agility and efficiency.

However, as business leaders venture into the realm of AI, understanding **ethics and transparency** becomes paramount. While AI wields the potential for transformative growth, it also demands a steadfast commitment to ethical standards. Ensuring transparency in AI-driven decisions fosters trust and safeguards an organization's reputation.

To navigate the rich tapestry of AI concepts effectively, organizational learning remains indispensable. Businesses must cultivate a culture that embraces continuous learning and experimentation. **Interdisciplinary collaboration** is key—melding expertise from data science, industry domains, and strategy to innovate and adapt in this fast-paced environment.

Mastering these concepts requires not only technical acumen but also strategic foresight and adaptability.

Embracing AI calls for a delicate balance of human insight and technological prowess.

The boundless potential of AI lies within its ability to intertwine with the intricacies of human decision-making. As these key concepts evolve, they extend beyond mere technological advances; they invite a revolutionary shift in how businesses operate, compete, and thrive.

Understanding these foundational concepts isn't just an academic exercise—it's a strategic imperative. For leaders equipped with this knowledge, the path forward is not just about adopting AI but orchestrating its profound impact on their organization's future. In doing so, they don't just adapt to the changing landscape—they lead it.

Data as the New Oil

The metaphor of data as the new oil has gained traction in recent years, and it's not hard to see why. In the digital age, data is the lifeblood of AI-powered decision-making. Just as oil was the driver of the industrial revolution, data is fueling the digital revolution, offering unprecedented opportunities for businesses to harness AI to make smarter, faster, and more informed decisions.

Consider this: every single day, massive amounts of data are generated from a multitude of sources—social media, IoT devices, customer transactions, and more. This data, when efficiently collected and properly analyzed, can provide insights that were previously unimaginable. It allows businesses to understand market trends, predict consumer behavior, and streamline operations. In essence, data empowers businesses to anticipate shifts and react with agility.

However, raw data is much like crude oil. It requires refining to be valuable. In the case of data, this means cleaning, processing, and analyzing it to extract actionable insights. The quality of insights directly correlates with the quality of data; thus, ensuring data accuracy and relevance is paramount. Businesses need robust data management strategies to sift through the noise and draw meaningful conclusions.

Data-driven decision-making doesn't simply involve collecting all the data available. It necessitates a strategic approach to determine which data is most relevant to specific business needs. Effective AI systems rely on the right data—data that is timely, accurate, and comprehensive. Without this, even the most sophisticated AI models will struggle to deliver valuable outputs.

The transformation of data into a valuable asset involves several key processes. Data collection is the first step, but it's critical to ensure that data is not just accumulated but curated. Storing data in a structured and accessible manner is essential for efficient analysis. This requires an investment in data storage technologies that can scale with the business's growth and evolving needs.

The next step in refining data is ensuring its quality. Data quality issues, such as duplicates, inconsistencies, and inaccuracies, can severely undermine AI efforts. Implementing data governance frameworks helps ensure data integrity and fosters trust in AI-generated insights. Businesses must prioritize data cleaning and validation processes to prevent errors and biases that could skew decision-making.

Once data is cleaned and validated, the analytical phase begins. AI technologies, particularly machine learning algorithms, rely on high-quality data to identify patterns and make predictions. The relationship between the AI systems and data is symbiotic; without data, machine learning models cannot learn, and without learning, they cannot improve or provide value.

Significantly, data's value extends beyond internal benefits. Data-driven insights can also enhance customer relationships and experiences. By understanding consumer behavior patterns, businesses can tailor their offerings to meet customer needs more effectively, leading to increased satisfaction and loyalty. Personalization becomes a powerful tool, drawing customers closer through bespoke experiences powered by data insights.

As data continues to permeate every aspect of modern business operations, it has created a new ecosystem where data privacy and security have become critical considerations. With great power comes great responsibility—businesses must navigate the complexities of data regulations and ensure that data handling practices comply with legal standards. Protecting customer data is not just a legal obligation but a cornerstone of maintaining trust and credibility in the AI era.

The competitive advantage offered by data-empowered AI cannot be overstated. Businesses that leverage high-quality data to feed sophisticated AI models are better positioned to lead in their respective industries. Data provides a lens into the future, allowing companies to foresee trends and make proactive decisions rather than reactive ones. This foresight can lead to innovations that redefine markets and disrupt traditional business models.

The metaphor of data as the new oil also highlights the global and strategic dimensions of data. Just as nations once competed for access to oil reserves, the digital economy is now characterized by a race to acquire, protect, and utilize data assets. Companies are investing heavily in data-driven technologies, recognizing that leadership in this arena can position them as industry pioneers.

However, the abundance of data presents its own set of challenges. The need for data scientists and analysts has surged as companies recognize the importance of extracting value from data. Building a skilled workforce capable of harnessing AI's potential requires investment in education and training.

Moreover, the rapid pace at which data is generated demands a continuous evolution of data strategies. Companies must remain agile, adapting to new data sources, analytics tools, and regulatory environments. Robust analytical capabilities and a culture that values data-driven insights are essential for maintaining an edge in a competitive landscape.

In conclusion, the concept of data as the new oil encapsulates the transformative power of data in AI-powered decision-making. Like oil, data's raw potential requires refinement to unlock its true value. Businesses that excel in data management and analytics will find themselves at the forefront of innovation, leveraging insights to drive strategic advantages and fuel growth. As the digital landscape evolves, the ability to harness data will distinguish leaders from laggards in the race to shape the future of business.

Chapter 3:
AI Tools and Technologies

Venturing into the landscape of AI tools and technologies unveils a dynamic world of innovation that offers business leaders powerful instruments to enhance decision-making and competitiveness. This chapter explores the burgeoning variety of AI solutions tailored to meet diverse business requirements. From robust machine learning platforms that drive predictive analytics to intuitive natural language processing tools that transform unstructured data into strategic insights, the toolkit is both vast and versatile. Knowing which tools align with your organization's unique goals is crucial; this selection process can significantly impact efficiency and strategic leverage. As you navigate this evolving ecosystem, staying informed about the latest advancements and understanding key functionalities can empower you to harness AI's full potential, driving transformative growth and establishing a competitive edge in an increasingly data-driven world.

Overview of Popular AI Tools

In today's rapidly evolving digital landscape, Artificial Intelligence (AI) is not just a buzzword—it's a strategic imperative. For business leaders keen on staying ahead, understanding popular AI tools is akin to owning a compass in uncharted territory. This section seeks to empower professionals with an overview of these essential tools, laying the groundwork for effective AI integration.

Often, the exploration of AI tools begins with machine learning platforms. One of the most prevalent in this domain is TensorFlow, developed by Google. It's an open-source platform renowned for its flexibility and comprehensive ecosystem that facilitates the development and deployment of machine learning models. Likewise, PyTorch, another significant player spearheaded by Facebook's AI Research lab, has captured the attention of researchers and developers alike for its usability and dynamic computational graph. These tools offer the backbone for businesses looking to harness the predictive powers of AI.

Beyond these platforms, businesses are finding immense value in data analytics tools that process vast amounts of information to derive actionable insights. Tableau, for instance, is a leading tool in data visualization, giving users the power to see and understand data in ways that are both intuitive and visually appealing. Similarly, Power BI by Microsoft delivers business analytics services with interactive visualizations and business intelligence capabilities, allowing an organization to make informed decisions swiftly.

Natural Language Processing (NLP) has revolutionized how machines understand human language. Tools such as Google's Cloud NLP and IBM's Watson are at the forefront of this technology, enabling businesses to analyze text for sentiment, extract entities, and more. They are pivotal for companies seeking to enhance customer experience through chatbot development, sentiment analysis, and language translation services, thus offering a more personalized consumer interaction.

For businesses keen on enhancing operational efficiencies, intelligent automation platforms such as UiPath, Blue Prism, and Automation Anywhere come into play. These tools facilitate robotic process automation (RPA), allowing businesses to automate repetitive, rule-based processes. By doing so, they free up human resources for more strategic tasks, driving efficiency and cost reduction.

Cloud-based AI solutions have seen a surge in adoption, with services like Google Cloud AI, Azure AI, and Amazon's AWS AI leading the charge. These platforms provide the necessary infrastructure and tools for businesses to develop AI applications without the burden of managing hardware resources. Their pay-as-you-go pricing model also offers flexibility and scalability, ensuring businesses can adjust their usage in line with their demand.

As AI becomes more ingrained in business strategies, the need for comprehensive, integrated AI suites grows. Salesforce Einstein and IBM Watson Studio represent examples of integrated solutions offering a range of AI functionalities across different business processes—from sales forecasting to customer service personalization. Such tools exemplify how AI can be seamlessly woven into the fabric of daily business operations.

In the domain of computer vision, OpenCV has been a game-changer. This tool allows for real-time image processing, which can be utilized in applications ranging from facial recognition to quality inspection in manufacturing. The capabilities it offers enable organizations to leverage AI for improving product quality and customer satisfaction.

AI in the enterprise setting is often tied to data—an organization's most valuable asset. Effective data management and integration platforms, such as Apache Hadoop and Apache Spark, are indispensable for handling big data. These tools offer distributed computing capabilities, ensuring that data-driven AI models are both robust and scalable.

Exploring these AI tools isn't just about technological acquisition; it's about aligning them with business strategies to unlock untapped potential. As companies integrate these tools, they foster environments where AI serves not only to automate and optimize but also to innovate and lead to new business models and opportunities.

In conclusion, by harnessing the power of these popular AI tools, business leaders can drive transformative change. The journey into AI is not just a technological venture but a strategic evolution. These tools are the enablers, providing the scaffolding to build innovative, data-driven, efficient organizations ready to tackle tomorrow's challenges.

Selecting the Right Tools for Your Business

In today's rapidly evolving technology landscape, selecting the right AI tools for your business means balancing immediate needs with future goals. It's not just about adopting the latest and greatest technology; it's about choosing tools that align strategically with your business objectives and add genuine value. Whether you manage a sprawling corporation or a nimble startup, identifying tools that integrate seamlessly into your existing systems—and can scale as your business grows—is crucial. The right tools are those that empower your teams, improve operational efficiency, and ultimately lead to smarter decision-making.

Start by assessing your organization's specific needs. What problems are you trying to solve? Is it about optimizing supply chain logistics, enhancing customer engagement, or improving data analytics? Understanding the exact challenges faced by your business aids in narrowing down the plethora of tools available. It's not uncommon to face analysis paralysis given the vast array of AI tools on the market. A clear articulation of your goals acts as a compass, guiding you through this complex terrain. Keep these goals front and center as you evaluate each potential solution.

Consult with cross-functional teams to gain a holistic view of your organizational needs. Your marketing department might prioritize a tool that offers deep insights into consumer behavior, while your operations team might be on the lookout for a system that can streamline processes. Engaging a diverse set of internal stakeholders not only aids in comprehensive need assessment but also fosters early buy-in from teams who will eventually use these AI tools. Open dialogues about requirements help prevent the adoption of siloed solutions that don't address interconnected business needs.

Once your needs are clear, consider the impact of AI tool integration on your existing business processes and technology stack. Are these tools compatible with current systems, or will they require extensive modifications? Seamless integration minimizes disruptions and accelerates the transition to new technologies. Pay attention to how easily these tools can mesh with your current infrastructure and technology landscape. Also, consider the learning curve for your employees; tools that are intuitive and user-friendly will save time in training and implementation, thereby providing faster returns on investment.

Don't overlook the importance of flexibility and scalability. Businesses today operate in environments characterized by rapid change and unpredictability. The AI tools you choose should adapt to new requirements as your business grows and evolves. Scalable solutions ensure you won't outgrow the technology as your enterprise expands. Flexibility allows your organization to pivot swiftly in response to market shifts, maintaining a competitive edge.

As you vet potential AI tools, prioritize those that stand out for their reliability and security. Reliable tools will perform consistently and accurately, thereby fostering trust within your organization. Similarly, security is paramount—especially when dealing with sensitive data. Ensure that the vendors you consider offer robust security protocols and data protection standards. A data breach could not only affect your business's bottom line but also erode stakeholder trust, an invaluable asset in today's digital age.

Vendor evaluation should also be a crucial part of the tool selection process. A strong partnership with your AI tool provider can make a significant difference in post-deployment support and ongoing innovation. Investigate potential vendors thoroughly: What's their track record? How do they handle customer service and support? Are they responsive to updates and improvements? Engaging with a vendor who is not just a provider but a partner can ease the intricacies of implementation and scaling.

While it's crucial to focus on current needs, keep an eye on future trends and advancements in AI technology. This foresight will help ensure that the tools you select remain relevant in the long term. Tools that are built on cutting-edge technologies like machine learning algorithms or natural language processing can provide a competitive advantage, preparing your business for future disruptions and innovations.

Finally, consider the cost implications, not just in terms of the initial outlay but also ongoing operational expenses. Total cost of ownership should factor into your decision-making process. By evaluating both short-term and long-term costs, you can better understand the financial commitment associated with each potential tool. While cost is a critical factor, it should not be the sole driver of your decisions. Sometimes, the value derived from more expensive but thoroughly effective tools justifies the investment, providing long-term benefits that outweigh financial considerations.

Selecting the right AI tools for your business can be as transformative as it is challenging. An informed, strategic approach ensures that your organization not only keeps pace with technological advancements but thrives in them. By understanding your needs, ensuring compatibility, emphasizing scalability, and opting for security, your enterprise will be well-equipped to leverage AI that enhances its competitive advantage. This choice, grounded in strategic foresight and aligned motivation, is not simply an investment in technology, but an investment in a sustainable future.

Chapter 4:
Building an AI Strategy

Crafting an effective AI strategy is a pivotal step for any organization aiming to harness the transformative power of artificial intelligence. It starts with a clear alignment between AI capabilities and business goals, ensuring that AI initiatives drive meaningful impact across the enterprise. Consider AI as a compass guiding decision-makers towards data-driven insights and efficiencies, enhancing core competencies rather than replacing them. Establishing robust frameworks for AI implementation is crucial, as they provide the roadmap for integrating AI into the fabric of the business. These frameworks should encompass not only the technological infrastructure but also cultural readiness, governance structures, and ethical considerations. By cultivating a shared vision and fostering collaboration across departments, leaders can pave the way for AI to become a strategic ally. This harmonized approach not only catalyzes innovation but also positions the organization to seize competitive advantage in an evolving digital landscape. With AI, businesses are not just reacting to change—they are proactively shaping the future.

Aligning AI with Business Goals

In the modern business landscape, the integration of Artificial Intelligence (AI) into strategic planning is not just beneficial—it's essential. Companies across industries are waking up to the potential of AI to transform processes, enhance decision-making, and provide a competitive edge. Yet, for AI initiatives to be truly successful, they must be meticulously aligned with the company's overarching business goals.

To start aligning AI with business goals, a clear understanding of the company's vision and mission is paramount. These elements form the cornerstone of any strategic endeavor, including AI projects. The strategic alignment means AI should not be seen as an independent technology initiative, but as a critical component of the broader business strategy. When business leaders ensure AI projects are derived from and support the core mission, they harness its power to amplify what the company stands for.

A crucial step in this alignment process involves identifying specific business objectives that AI can help achieve. Whether it's increasing revenue, reducing costs, enhancing customer experiences, or improving operational efficiency, each objective should have a clear connection to an AI solution. For instance, leveraging AI for predictive analytics can offer invaluable insights that drive sales strategies or optimize inventory management, directly impacting business outcomes.

While it may seem tempting to adopt AI for its novelty, such an approach is fraught with risks. Instead, business leaders should focus on areas where AI aligns directly with their strategic priorities. It requires a keen understanding of the problems AI can solve and the unique capabilities it brings to the table. Engaging stakeholders from different departments can foster a holistic view of the organizational needs and how AI fits into the puzzle.

After establishing the potential of AI for achieving business goals, the next focus should be on resource allocation. Proper budgeting for AI projects is critical, and companies need to be prepared to make investments not only in technology but also in human capital. This includes upskilling current employees and recruiting AI experts who can guide the strategic implementation of AI technologies within the organization.

Moreover, metrics and Key Performance Indicators (KPIs) must be established from the outset. These metrics will serve as benchmarks for assessing the performance and impact of AI initiatives in relation to business goals. By tracking metrics such as cost savings, customer satisfaction levels, and productivity gains, companies can evaluate the effectiveness of their AI strategies and make data-driven adjustments as needed.

Feedback loops play a vital role in this continuous alignment process. The dynamic nature of AI and business environments necessitates ongoing evaluation and adjustment. Business leaders should foster a culture of feedback, leveraging insights from AI solutions to refine strategies and improve outcomes. This iterative process not only enhances alignment but also ensures AI systems remain relevant and effective over time.

It's also essential to create cross-functional teams that unite AI developers with business managers and domain experts. Such collaboration ensures the practicality and success of AI implementations. By combining diverse expertise, businesses can pinpoint the most valuable applications of AI, tailor solutions to specific needs, and foresee potential challenges before they escalate.

Furthermore, as AI technologies evolve, maintaining alignment with business goals requires an adaptable mindset. The strategic landscape constantly shifts; thus, AI initiatives must be flexible enough to pivot direction as necessary. Business leaders should encourage innovation and exploration within AI projects, advocating for a learning-oriented environment that mitigates risks and capitalizes on opportunities.

Finally, ethical considerations must not be overlooked. AI strategies should align not only with business goals but also with ethical standards and societal values. As AI systems often have profound impacts on both individuals and communities, companies are responsible for ensuring their AI practices uphold transparency, fairness, and accountability. This ethical alignment reinforces trust and credibility, evening the playing field for sustainable success.

In conclusion, aligning AI with business goals is a multifaceted endeavor. It demands a strategic lens that views AI as an integral part of the business narrative. With thoughtful planning, alignment fosters innovation, drives mission-critical objectives, and places companies at the forefront of their industries. When executed effectively, AI doesn't just support business goals—it propels them forward, positioning the organization for sustained success in an increasingly competitive marketplace.

Frameworks for AI Implementation

In the journey of integrating AI into a business strategy, "Frameworks for AI Implementation" is a crucial section. It serves as the bridge from conceptual understanding and goal alignment to tangible execution. Frameworks provide a structured approach to deploying AI, ensuring that initiatives are grounded, scalable, and sustainable. They offer a roadmap for businesses, illuminating the path from ideation to action.

When considering AI implementation, one must first evaluate the organization's readiness. This evaluation involves an introspective analysis of existing resources, competencies, and culture. Leaders should ask: Is the organizational data infrastructure robust enough to support AI? Are there skilled personnel who can steward these technologies? It's essential to cultivate a culture that embraces innovation and change, where teams are encouraged to think creatively and adopt new technologies.

One popular framework in AI implementation is the CRISP-DM methodology, originally developed for data mining projects but highly applicable here. CRISP-DM stands for Cross-Industry Standard Process for Data Mining. It includes six phases: business understanding, data understanding, data preparation, modeling, evaluation, and deployment. Each phase is critical in the AI deployment cycle, offering a systematic view that can prevent common pitfalls and guide organizations through complex processes. By maintaining a clear focus on business objectives, this framework helps ensure that the AI solutions developed are aligned with the strategic goals.

Another approach is the "Agile" methodology, widely used in software development. Agile encourages adaptive planning, evolutionary development, and early delivery. It allows teams to rapidly iterate through cycles, incorporating feedback and learning from each iteration. In the context of AI, this means being able to test hypotheses, assess models, and refine solutions based on real-world performance. Agile promotes cross-functional collaboration, ensuring that diverse perspectives contribute to the implementation process.

AI frameworks must also consider governance and ethics from the outset. Ensuring the responsible use of AI requires establishing oversight mechanisms and ethical guidelines. Frameworks that integrate ethical considerations can prevent the deployment of biased models or applications that infringe on privacy. This alignment is vital; it fosters trust and ensures compliance with emerging regulations, an aspect no business leader can afford to overlook.

Additionally, frameworks like the AI Canvas provide a visual and strategic tool for exploring AI opportunities. The AI Canvas helps organizations to articulate the value proposition of AI initiatives clearly, map out data requirements, understand the user journey, and anticipate constraints and potential risks. By visually documenting the journey, teams can better communicate and share insights, facilitating stronger alignment across business units.

Implementing AI also requires a harmonized focus on technology and talent. While the former involves hardware, software, and data infrastructure, the latter is about skills, training, and organizational culture. The modern workforce needs upskilling to work effectively alongside AI technologies. This element of AI frameworks involves identifying skill gaps and investing in education programs to bridge these gaps. Empowering employees with AI knowledge not only improves morale but also enhances innovation and accelerates adoption.

Another strategic framework focuses on collaborative partnerships. Many businesses achieve AI success by partnering with technology companies, academic institutions, or startups. These collaborations can accelerate innovation, offering access to cutting-edge research and development technology that might otherwise be inaccessible. Many partnerships operate as ecosystems where ideas, tools, and practices flow freely across institutional boundaries, enriching the AI implementation process.

Moreover, frameworks emphasize the significance of continuous improvement and scalability. AI projects should never remain static; they must evolve based on feedback and changing business needs. Frameworks must allow for iterative enhancements, ensuring that solutions adapt to new data patterns and market dynamics. Scalability ensures that as projects mature, they can expand seamlessly within the organization, delivering increasing value over time.

To close, it's essential to mention that frameworks in AI implementation are not rigid blueprints. They serve as guides that can be tailored to fit unique organizational contexts. Companies should view these frameworks as living documents, evolving as technologies advance and organizational priorities shift. By leveraging such strategic frameworks, businesses can navigate the complexities of AI adoption, driving sustainable growth and gaining a competitive advantage.

Chapter 5:
Data Management for AI

In today's digital economy, data management is the linchpin for leveraging AI's transformative potential within any organization. Properly handled data provides a solid foundation for AI-driven strategies, ensuring they are both effective and sustainable. Systems need to capture a diverse array of data precisely and securely, with a storage architecture that can handle dynamic scaling as businesses grow. To maximize AI's benefits, it's crucial to maintain high data quality, achieving accuracy, completeness, and relevance, to avoid flawed insights or suboptimal decisions. Business leaders must champion the continuous evolution of data management strategies, fostering an environment where technology seamlessly integrates with business processes, amplifying both efficiency and innovation. Such diligent practice prepares organizations not only to capitalize on current AI opportunities but also to stay ahead in an ever-evolving competitive landscape.

Data Collection and Storage

In today's data-driven world, effective data collection and storage are not just integral to AI development; they are the bedrock upon which successful AI strategies are built. This section delves into the nuances of collecting and storing data with precision and foresight, a foundational component for any business aiming to harness the power of Artificial Intelligence effectively. It demands not just technical adeptness but also strategic vision.

Understanding the intricacies of data collection isn't merely about capturing as much data as possible. It's about ensuring that the data you collect is relevant, timely, and actionable. In the AI context, data serves as the raw material for deriving insights and driving intelligent decision-making. Hence, starting with a clear understanding of what data is required to meet business objectives is crucial. Companies should define clear parameters of what constitutes valuable data, ensuring alignment with strategic goals and anticipated AI uses.

The process of data collection involves a multitude of sources. Traditional sources such as customer transactions, operational logs, and financial records are augmented by new-age data streams emerging from IoT devices, social media interactions, and mobile applications. Businesses must carefully select sources to provide comprehensive insights, enhancing the diversity and richness of data necessary for sophisticated AI models. Additionally, businesses can utilize external data streams like market trends and demographic statistics to complement internal data. This combination can create a more holistic view and provide deeper insights.

Effective data storage isn't just about haphazard accumulation. It's about organizing and structuring data to be easily accessible and usable. With the staggering volumes of data that organizations generate, cloud-based storage solutions have become indispensable. They offer scalability, flexibility, and cost-effectiveness compared to traditional data centers. Businesses can adapt storage needs to data demands, paying only for what they use. Furthermore, distributed storage solutions enhance redundancy, ensuring data availability even in cases of localized failures.

Data storage solutions have evolved with technology, and cloud architecture is at the forefront of this transformation. Cloud providers offer infrastructures that not only store data but also integrate advanced analytics capabilities. This integration facilitates seamless data movement between storage and analysis stages, accelerating processing times and reducing complexities.

A significant challenge in data management is ensuring data integrity and security. As data volume increases, so does the risk of breaches and unauthorized access. Businesses must implement robust security protocols, including encryption, access controls, and regular audits to safeguard data assets. Compliance with regulations such as GDPR and CCPA also implicates how data is collected, stored, and utilized by organizations. These regulations aim to protect consumer data privacy and implement strict penalties for non-compliance, making adherence a critical component of data management strategies.

Moreover, the concept of data governance has emerged as an essential framework for managing data assets. By defining policies around data usage, responsibility, and compliance, businesses can streamline processes and minimize risks. Data governance ensures that all data-related activities align with broader organizational objectives while maintaining high standards of quality and security. Establishing a governance model involves assigning roles and responsibilities, defining data standards, and setting procedures for data lifecycle management.

As AI technologies advance, the emphasis on structured and unstructured data has shifted. While traditional databases excel at managing structured data, most information generated today, including text, images, and videos, is unstructured. Consequently, businesses should invest in specialized databases and technologies capable of efficiently processing diverse data types. Technologies such as graph databases and NoSQL engines offer flexible solutions for handling unstructured and highly interconnected data.

Data cleaning and preprocessing are critical steps in transforming raw data into a usable format for AI applications. Data in its raw form is often incomplete, inconsistent, and noisy. Processes like data cleansing, normalization, and transformation help identify and rectify such issues. These procedures involve standardizing data formats, identifying missing values, and correcting inaccuracies. A meticulous preprocessing phase ensures that AI models receive high-quality inputs, improving their performance and accuracy.

Furthermore, businesses must establish clear protocols for data lifecycle management. Managing data throughout its lifecycle—from creation and storage to archiving and deletion—helps maintain data relevance and usability. It also ensures compliance with legal requirements concerning data retention and disposal. Businesses should develop strategies to determine when data is no longer useful and can be securely deleted, reducing storage costs and minimizing cybersecurity risks.

An emerging trend in data management is the incorporation of machine learning techniques to automate data collection and storage processes. AI models can intelligently categorize and annotate data, recognizing patterns that enhance data quality and utility. This automation reduces manual intervention, accelerates processing, and allows human resources to focus on strategic analysis rather than routine tasks. Leveraging AI technologies for data management brings efficiencies and paves the way for more adaptive and responsive systems.

In conclusion, businesses aiming to integrate AI into their operations must place significant emphasis on crafting a robust data collection and storage strategy. The journey from data creation to actionable insights involves meticulous planning, investment in appropriate technologies, and adherence to regulatory standards. By focusing on these aspects, companies can ensure that data serves as a powerful enabler, driving innovation, competitiveness, and the successful application of AI-driven strategies.

Ensuring Data Quality

Data is the lifeblood of artificial intelligence systems. For AI to deliver accurate and reliable insights, the quality of the data it processes cannot be underestimated. Ensuring data quality is about much more than just data cleaning. It's about establishing trust in the data-driven decisions AI can facilitate, allowing businesses to confidently align their strategies with insights derived from AI technologies.

At the core of data quality lies the concept of **accuracy**. It's essential for data to correctly represent the real-world scenario it describes. If erroneous or incomplete data enters an AI system, it can lead to flawed predictions and misguided decisions. Thus, maintaining accuracy is paramount. This often requires implementing meticulous data validation procedures and robust error-checking mechanisms to catch anomalies before they skew the AI outcomes.

Another critical aspect of data quality is **consistency**. Inconsistent data results in unreliable analysis and interpretations. Standardizing data formats and ensuring uniform data collection methods across the organization are steps toward achieving consistency. When data is gathered using varied methodologies, even the most sophisticated AI systems struggle to reconcile differences, leading to errors in insight generation.

Besides accuracy and consistency, **completeness** is a key factor in ensuring data quality. Incomplete data can directly affect the outcome of AI predictions and analyses. Businesses need comprehensive data protocols that ensure all relevant data is captured across channels. This task becomes even more complex with unstructured data, where completeness isn't simply about filling in missing fields but about ensuring that all meaningful information is extracted and utilized.

Yet, ensuring data quality isn't limited to assessing the data's inherent attributes. **Timeliness** is equally crucial. In the fast-paced world of business, data that's accurate today might become irrelevant tomorrow. Therefore, ensuring data freshness by regularly updating datasets is vital. Outdated data can mislead AI models, resulting in business strategies that are out of sync with current circumstances.

Turning our attention to **relevance**, not all data is created equal in terms of its applicability to a given AI task. The challenge often lies in filtering out noise—data that is correct but not useful for the particular analysis at hand. Businesses must define clear criteria for data relevance, ensuring that only pertinent information is harnessed for AI processes. This can significantly enhance the efficiency and effectiveness of an organization's AI efforts.

Organizational data management practices must also emphasize the importance of **contextual integrity**. Data in isolation can lead to misinterpretation. Understanding the context—such as the conditions under which the data was collected and the intended audience—is crucial. This relevance to context ensures that AI systems can interpret data accurately, applying it to scenarios that align with business needs.

Ensuring data quality involves a comprehensive strategy that includes **data governance**. This involves setting policies and standards for data usage and access, which helps in maintaining data integrity across the enterprise. Strong governance frameworks outline who can access data, under what conditions, and for what purposes. This safeguards sensitive information and ensures compliance with regulatory requirements, which is becoming increasingly important amid growing data privacy concerns.

Data quality also relies on **technological infrastructure**. Leveraging the right tools and technologies can enhance data quality management. From traditional ETL (extract, transform, load) tools to modern cloud-based platforms, businesses have numerous options.

Choosing the right tools that align with an organization's specific data management needs can streamline data quality processes, ensuring that AI systems receive the best possible input data.

Furthermore, human oversight is indispensable in maintaining data quality. Automated systems can do much, but they're not infallible. Including human expertise in the loop helps identify subtle data issues that might elude even the most advanced algorithms. Training and empowering employees to recognize and value data quality is a cultural shift that encourages vigilance across all levels of data interaction.

Finally, in the realm of AI, **feedback loops** represent a dynamic approach to data quality management. As AI systems generate outcomes, their accuracy can be evaluated over time. This feedback can be used to refine data quality, identifying patterns or anomalies that may suggest issues in the datasets used. This iterative approach not only improves the quality of the data but also enhances the subsequent efficacy of AI models.

As business leaders keen on leveraging AI for strategic advantage, ensuring data quality is a non-negotiable component of AI deployment. It requires a proactive approach, involving a blend of technology, policy, and human judgment. While it might seem daunting, investing in data quality fosters a robust foundation for reliable AI solutions, ultimately leading to more accurate, insightful decision-making and significant competitive advantage.

Chapter 6:
Machine Learning and Analytics

As we delve into the transformative world of machine learning and analytics, we stand at the crossroads of strategic opportunity and technological advancement. Machine learning, a pivotal subset of AI, empowers businesses to uncover patterns and insights from data that were previously unimaginable. By employing predictive analytics, companies can now anticipate customer behavior, optimize operational efficiencies, and tailor strategies with unprecedented precision. For business leaders, this chapter is a call to harness these capabilities not merely as tools, but as essential pillars in decision-making processes, shaping a future where insights drive action. In embracing this, you're not only positioning your organization at the forefront of innovation but also forging a path toward sustained competitive advantage. With machine learning and analytics, the potential to redefine market landscapes and customer experiences is truly boundless, empowering you to make informed and strategic decisions that are deeply anchored in data-driven insights.

Fundamentals of Machine Learning

Machine learning is a cornerstone of artificial intelligence that transforms how businesses operate and compete. At its core, machine learning is about building systems capable of learning from data. This involves designing algorithms that can make predictions or decisions based on past experiences or identified patterns. For business leaders, understanding these fundamentals isn't just desirable—it's essential for strategic decision-making.

To appreciate why machine learning is so pivotal, consider how it contrasts with traditional programming. In conventional software, we hard-code instructions for the computer to follow. With machine learning, however, the computer learns from examples instead of being explicitly programmed for every possible scenario. This capability allows companies to analyze vast datasets and glean insights that were previously unattainable.

One fundamental aspect of machine learning is its reliance on data. The more data an algorithm can access, the better it can learn and generalize. It's the abundance of data that fuels modern machine learning models, making them more accurate and efficient. As a business professional, you should recognize data not only as a resource but as a powerful strategic asset that can drive innovation and competitive advantage.

Machine learning models come in various flavors, primarily categorized into supervised and unsupervised learning. Supervised learning involves training a model on a labeled dataset, teaching it to predict an output from given inputs. This approach is widely used in applications like email filtering and quality control. Unsupervised learning, on the other hand, identifies hidden patterns or intrinsic structures in input data without explicit labels, which is useful in market segmentation and anomaly detection.

The complexity of machine learning models can vary significantly. Some models, like linear regression, offer straightforward interpretations and are easy to use, making them valuable for clear and direct applications. Others involve layered systems of learning, such as neural networks, which can uncover deep insights but require more data and computational power. Each has its place and application depending on the business context.

Feature engineering is another crucial element in the success of machine learning models. It involves selecting and transforming data attributes to improve the predictive power of the model. Business practitioners often leverage domain knowledge to ensure features align correctly with business realities and outcomes. The art of feature selection and transformation can dramatically affect a model's performance, highlighting the tight integration needed between data science and business expertise.

Moreover, business professionals must grasp the concept of overfitting and underfitting. An overfitted model learns the training data too well, capturing noise alongside the signal, which reduces its ability to generalize to new data. Conversely, an underfitted model is too simplistic to capture the underlying trend of the data. Balancing this delicate act is key to building models that are both robust and reliable.

Machine learning isn't just about models learning from data; it's also about continuously adjusting and improving those models. The lifecycle of a machine learning project involves ongoing iteration and enhancement. This adaptability is what makes machine learning such a powerful tool in the fast-paced world of business, where change is constant, and agility is a non-negotiable trait.

Lastly, the integration of machine learning into business processes requires a cultural mindset shift. It involves fostering a data-driven culture where insights derived from machine learning influence strategic decisions and operational tactics. By harnessing these insights effectively, organizations can transform processes, enhance customer experiences, and create a sustainable competitive edge.

In summary, understanding the fundamentals of machine learning goes beyond technical know-how—it's about recognizing its strategic impact on business. By leveraging machine learning, leaders can unlock new opportunities, drive efficiency, and set the stage for lasting innovation. As you move forward, it's imperative to keep exploring and experimenting with these technologies to stay ahead in an increasingly competitive landscape.

Applying Predictive Analytics

In the realm of machine learning and analytics, predictive analytics stands out as a transformative tool. It's not just about forecasting the future; it's about reshaping business decision-making. Predictive analytics involves using historical data, machine learning algorithms, and statistical methods to forecast future events. For business leaders, this means transforming data into actionable insights. It's no longer enough to react to trends; successful organizations are now predicting and shaping them.

The crux of predictive analytics lies in its ability to change the very fabric of strategic planning. By understanding patterns and trends in past data, businesses can foresee potential opportunities and threats. This forward-thinking approach equips decision-makers to be proactive, rather than reactive. For instance, by predicting customer behavior, companies can tailor their products and marketing strategies to better meet consumer demands, thereby gaining a competitive edge.

One of the key advantages of predictive analytics is its versatility. It can be applied across various domains, from optimizing supply chains to enhancing marketing strategies. In finance, for example, predictive models can anticipate market shifts and guide investment strategies accordingly. Operations can be streamlined, minimizing waste and improving efficiency, by predicting demand surges and aligning production capacity with these forecasts.

At its core, predictive analytics involves three main components: data collection, analytical algorithms, and deployment processes. First, data collection requires gathering and curating relevant datasets, which is foundational for any analysis. Without high-quality data, even the most sophisticated models can yield inaccurate predictions. Ensuring data integrity and relevance is thus a non-negotiable step.

Next, the analytical algorithms come into play. These algorithms, powered by machine learning, sift through volumes of data to identify patterns and correlations that might not be visible to the human eye. Techniques such as regression analysis, time series analysis, and neural networks are commonly employed. These algorithms are the brains behind predictive analytics, turning massive datasets into digestible insights.

But having great data and powerful algorithms isn't the entire equation. Deployment processes ensure that predictive insights are incorporated into everyday business decisions. This means integrating analytics seamlessly into existing workflows, which often requires a shift in corporate culture and mindset. Decision-makers must grow comfortable with, and trusting of, the insights provided by machines—a transformation that involves both technical adjustments and emotional shifts.

However, applying predictive analytics isn't without its challenges. Data privacy and security remain paramount concerns. Handlers of sensitive information must navigate compliance with regulations like GDPR or CCPA while maintaining the integrity and confidentiality of their datasets. Ensuring ethical data use, tackling potential biases in data or algorithms, and building transparent models are essential steps to foster trust among stakeholders.

The complexity of implementing predictive analytics also extends to technical expertise. Aligning the goals of data scientists with business objectives requires a cross-disciplinary approach. Businesses must foster collaborations between technical teams and domain experts to ensure that predictions align with strategic goals and create value. Organizations can cultivate internal talent or partner with external specialists to build a robust predictive analytics framework.

Yet, the transformative potential of predictive analytics shouldn't be stifled by these challenges. As more industries recognize its power, we're seeing predictive analytics being used to foster innovation. In healthcare, for instance, predicting patient admissions can optimize staffing and improve patient care. Retailers can use it to forecast inventory needs and reduce the risk of stockouts or overstocking, fine-tuning the balance between supply and demand.

Moreover, the application of predictive analytics is not confined to corporations with vast resources. Small and Medium Enterprises (SMEs) stand to benefit tremendously, given their agility and capacity for quick adaptation. These enterprises can access cloud-based predictive analytics tools that are scalable and cost-effective, bypassing the need for heavy capital investment.

The future of predictive analytics in business is promising, with advancements in artificial intelligence and machine learning continuing to expand its capabilities. Real-time analytics, fueled by the influx of data from IoT devices, is shifting predictive analytics from a backward-looking exercise to a real-time, dynamic decision-making tool.

As this field continues to evolve, business leaders should view predictive analytics not just as a tool but as an integral part of their strategic arsenal. By championing a data-driven culture, organizations can harness these predictive insights to navigate uncertainties and steer toward long-term success.

Ultimately, the true power of predictive analytics lies in its ability to empower business professionals to see the invisible and forecast the unimaginable. As businesses continue to innovate and evolve in this fast-paced digital world, predictive analytics will undoubtedly play an indispensable role in shaping strategies and driving sustainable growth.

Chapter 7:
AI in Marketing

In the rapidly evolving landscape of digital commerce, AI in marketing has become a game-changer, offering unprecedented personalization and customer insights that were once unattainable. By analyzing mountains of data, AI learns consumer behavior, allowing businesses to craft messages and experiences tailored uniquely to individual preferences. This level of personalization boosts customer engagement, fosters brand loyalty, and drives sales conversion rates. Additionally, AI optimizes marketing campaigns by identifying patterns and predicting trends with remarkable accuracy. This enables marketers to allocate resources more efficiently and adjust strategies in real-time. As AI continues to advance, its integration into marketing not only enhances the consumer journey but also equips businesses to stay ahead in a competitive marketplace, redefining how they connect and communicate with their audiences.

Personalization and Customer Insights

Personalization in marketing isn't just a buzzword anymore; it's the modus operandi for any enterprise keen to stay relevant in today's dynamic marketplace. The traditional one-size-fits-all approach in marketing has swiftly become obsolete. Businesses are realizing the transformative potential of personalization powered by AI, which helps them understand customers more deeply and engage them more effectively.

At the core of AI-driven personalization is the ability to analyze vast amounts of customer data in real-time. AI excels at processing diverse data sets—from browsing patterns and purchase histories to social media activity and even offline interactions. Through this analysis, AI can identify patterns and insights that were previously inaccessible. These insights enable a business to tailor its messaging, offer personalized product recommendations, and even predict future behaviors. This kind of in-depth understanding is pivotal for crafting personalized customer experiences that truly resonate.

One significant benefit of AI in personalization is real-time interaction. Advanced algorithms can adjust a company's marketing strategies on-the-fly, responding immediately to changes in customer behavior or market dynamics. Imagine a clothing retailer suggesting a new outfit not just based on a customer's past purchases, but also considering current weather conditions, upcoming travel plans, or recent fashion trends made possible through AI-driven forecasts. These instant, personalized responses foster a sense of connection, making customers feel valued and understood.

Another aspect where AI shines is in the segmentation of audiences. Instead of traditional broad-based demographic segmentations, AI allows for micro-segmentation, which clusters customers into highly defined segments. This granular segmentation is driven by sophisticated algorithms that analyze not just who the customers are, but how they behave in real-time. Micro-segmentation enables businesses to develop highly targeted marketing strategies, thereby increasing the chances of conversion.

The power of AI in personalization isn't just about understanding individual preferences but also predicting them. Predictive analytics, a branch of AI, takes center stage when it comes to anticipating the needs and desires of customers. By unraveling complex datasets, AI can forecast trends, identify future customer needs, and even predict potential churn. This proactive approach ensures that businesses can address customer concerns before they even arise, bolstering customer satisfaction and loyalty.

Customer insights derived from AI extend beyond marketing to influence product development, customer service, and sales strategies. Consider an AI system integrated with a customer service platform. It can analyze various interactions to identify common pain points, thereby revealing areas for product improvements or additional services. This holistic application of AI insights can guide a company not only in refining its products but also in maximizing its overall customer value proposition.

Furthermore, AI in personalization isn't restricted to just digital channels. Integrative AI solutions are capable of bridging offline and online data, creating a seamless customer experience across all touchpoints. Whether a customer walks into a store or browses a website, AI ensures that their preferences and history are understood and catered for. This omnichannel personalization is crucial in today's interconnected world, where customers often begin their purchasing journey in one channel and complete it in another.

Companies leveraging AI for personalization and insights must ensure they adhere to privacy regulations and maintain customer trust. Transparency about data usage and robust data security measures are paramount. It's crucial that businesses communicate how AI-driven personalization is enhancing their customers' experiences rather than simply using data for exploitation. Building trust in AI systems is not just an ethical concern but a strategic advantage, paving the way for long-term customer relationships.

As you integrate AI into your marketing strategy, fostering a culture of experimentation and learning is essential. Encouraging your team to harness AI technologies allows for creative experimentation in crafting personalized customer journeys, testing new methodologies, and iterating on successful strategies. These collaborative efforts fuel innovation and keep your brand agile amidst rapid technological advancements.

In conclusion, personalization and customer insights harnessed through AI are formidable tools for gaining a strategic edge in marketing. By leveraging AI, companies can transform customer interactions into meaningful engagements, drive business growth, and cultivate enduring customer loyalty. As digital landscapes continue to evolve, the ability to intimately know and predict your customers will be the beacon of competitive advantage. Push beyond the boundaries of traditional marketing and seize the opportunities that AI personalization presents. The journey toward deeper customer insights is not just transformative; it's imperative for success in the AI era.

Optimizing Marketing Campaigns

In the dynamic landscape of marketing, traditional approaches often fall short of delivering the desired impact. With the emergence of AI, marketing campaigns can now be optimized to achieve unprecedented levels of precision and effectiveness. AI offers a unique advantage in understanding and predicting consumer behavior, transforming how businesses reach and engage their audience.

AI-powered predictive analytics stand at the core of optimizing marketing campaigns. By analyzing vast amounts of data from diverse sources, AI models can foresee future trends and customer needs. This insight allows marketers to tailor their strategies and messages more effectively, ensuring that the right content reaches the right audience at the right time. It's more than just guesswork now; it's a data-driven approach that dramatically increases the probability of campaign success.

Another significant advantage of AI in marketing is the ability to automate tasks that were previously labor-intensive. Campaign management tools, powered by AI, can handle everything from social media scheduling to dynamic ad placements. With automation, marketers can focus more on strategic elements rather than getting bogged down in repetitive tasks. This not only saves time but also reduces the potential for human error, allowing campaigns to run smoother and more efficiently.

Personalization, a buzzword in modern marketing, takes on a whole new meaning with AI. Traditional segmentation strategies grouped audiences into relatively broad categories. AI, in contrast, allows for hyper-personalized campaigns by analyzing individual customer data in real-time. This level of customization can significantly improve conversion rates, as consumers are more likely to engage with content that resonates with their unique preferences and behaviors.

Moreover, AI can help optimize marketing budgets, ensuring that resources are allocated where they'll yield the most return. This optimization is achieved by utilizing sophisticated algorithms that assess the performance of various marketing channels and provide insights on where to invest more heavily. Businesses can effectively reduce wasteful spending and focus their efforts on the most productive strategies.

Testing and iterating campaign strategies traditionally required extensive time and effort. AI accelerates this process through simulation and modeling techniques. These approaches allow marketers to test different scenarios and predict outcomes before implementing them in the real world. This not only speeds up the decision-making process but also enhances the flexibility and adaptability of marketing campaigns.

AI also plays a pivotal role in content creation and development. Natural Language Processing (NLP) tools can generate high-quality copy for ads, emails, and social media posts, freeing up time for creative teams to focus on larger strategic decisions. AI can also curate content by identifying trending topics and delivering content that's most likely to capture user interest, thus maximizing engagement potential.

With all these advantages, integrating AI into marketing campaigns requires a strategic approach. Organizations must first ensure they have access to high-quality, relevant data. Without the right data, even the most advanced AI systems can produce ineffective results. Furthermore, selecting the right AI tools and technologies that align with business objectives is crucial. Each organization should evaluate their unique needs and goals to tailor their AI approach accordingly.

Change management is another critical component when optimizing marketing campaigns with AI. Teams need to be educated and trained on how to leverage these new technologies effectively. Resistance to change can often be a hurdle, so cultivating a culture that embraces innovation and continuous learning is essential for seamless AI integration.

The impact of AI on marketing is not just theoretical but evidenced by real-world successes. Companies that have adopted AI-driven marketing strategies report significant improvements in customer engagement and sales. These organizations have set themselves apart from competitors through improved customer insights and more agile campaign execution.

The future of marketing with AI promises even more revolutionary changes. As technologies like machine learning and AI continue to evolve, so will their applications in marketing. The potential for further innovations, such as using AI to understand emotional responses or conducting automatic A/B testing at scale, is vast and exciting.

In conclusion, optimizing marketing campaigns with AI is not merely an enhancement but a fundamental shift in strategy. It's about using the power of predictive analytics, automation, and personalization to convert potential customers into loyal advocates efficiently. As business leaders consider the integration of AI into their marketing efforts, they must embrace this transformative potential to gain a strategic advantage in today's competitive environment. The journey may be complex, but the rewards, both in terms of customer satisfaction and business performance, justify the effort.

Chapter 8:
AI in Operations Management

In the fast-evolving landscape of business operations, AI is proving to be a transformative force that transcends traditional boundaries. By integrating AI-driven solutions into operations management, businesses can streamline processes, enabling enhanced efficiency and productivity. AI's capabilities—ranging from predictive analytics to autonomous systems—allow organizations to optimize their supply chains, reducing costs and accelerating delivery times. Machine learning algorithms analyze vast amounts of operational data in real-time, uncovering patterns that humans might miss and proposing actionable insights. This empowers decision-makers to proactively address potential bottlenecks and adapt to changing demands swiftly. Consequently, AI becomes a vital tool not just for maintaining current operational standards but for setting new benchmarks in operational excellence, fostering a culture of innovation and continuous improvement.

Streamlining Processes with AI

In today's rapidly evolving business environment, the integration of Artificial Intelligence (AI) into operations management offers transformative potential. As organizations face increasing pressure to enhance operational efficiency and cut costs, AI emerges as a pivotal solution. Leveraging AI not only streamlines processes but also infuses operations with a level of intelligence that enables more agile decision-making.

One compelling advantage of AI in operations is its ability to seamlessly handle routine tasks, freeing up human resources for more strategic activities. For example, AI-powered automation in manufacturing can manage repetitive tasks such as assembly line sorting or quality checks, often with greater precision and speed than human workers. This shift allows human employees to focus on innovative problem-solving and strategic initiatives that drive the company forward.

Beyond mere automation, AI brings predictive capabilities to the forefront of operations management. Through machine learning algorithms, businesses can anticipate shifts in demand, optimize inventory levels, and adjust production schedules accordingly. This predictive power minimizes waste, reduces holding costs, and ensures that resources are allocated where they're most needed, thus improving the overall efficiency of the supply chain.

The implementation of AI in operational workflows also facilitates superior process optimization. By continuously analyzing large datasets, AI systems identify bottlenecks, inefficiencies, and opportunities for cost reduction. These insights allow managers to fine-tune processes in real-time, promoting a culture of continuous improvement. As a result, operations become more aligned with strategic business goals, enhancing both short-term outcomes and long-term viability.

Additionally, AI's impact extends to the realm of customer service operations. Intelligent chatbots and virtual assistants provide instant support to customers, handling inquiries and resolving issues with remarkable efficiency. As AI models learn from each interaction, they refine their responses, reducing the need for human intervention and offering a more consistent customer experience. This not only increases satisfaction but also frees customer service agents to manage more complex cases.

A key element of AI-driven process optimization is its ability to harness and operationalize data from disparate sources. Internet of Things (IoT) devices, for instance, generate vast streams of data that, when paired with AI analytics, offer insights into equipment performance and usage patterns. Proactive maintenance schedules, driven by these insights, help prevent costly downtime and extend the lifespan of machinery.

While the benefits are vast, implementing AI in operational processes requires a strategic approach. Organizations must ensure that they have the right infrastructure to support AI technologies, including robust data management systems. This typically involves grooming data for AI applications through rigorous cleaning, structuring, and storing processes. Ensuring data quality is pivotal, as AI models are only as effective as the data they are trained on.

Moreover, integrating AI into existing workflows often requires a cultural shift within organizations. Employees may need to adapt to new collaborative methods with AI systems, which may initially be met with resistance. However, through comprehensive training programs and a clear demonstration of AI's value, businesses can drive adoption and foster a workforce that is comfortable working alongside AI.

It's important to note that AI is not a one-size-fits-all solution. Customization is crucial to aligning AI capabilities with specific organizational needs and goals. Companies must carefully assess their operations to identify which processes are ripe for AI enhancement and tailor AI solutions accordingly.

Furthermore, transparency in AI operations is critical. As AI systems become more involved in decision-making, providing explanations of AI-driven outcomes builds trust with stakeholders. Transparent AI not only enhances decision-making but also ensures adherence to regulatory standards and ethical considerations.

In summary, AI is revolutionizing operations management by making processes more agile, intelligent, and efficient. By automating repetitive tasks, providing predictive insights, and optimizing workflows, AI empowers businesses to respond swiftly to market dynamics and customer demands. As AI technologies continue to evolve, their integration into operational processes will undoubtedly expand, offering even greater potential for innovation and competitive advantage. Embracing these advancements positions businesses to thrive in a future where AI is a cornerstone of operational excellence.

Enhancing Supply Chain Efficiency

As we delve deeper into the transformative impact of AI on operations management, one area that stands out significantly is the supply chain. AI's ability to enhance supply chain efficiency stems from its capacity to process large volumes of data and provide actionable insights in real time. It's not just about automating tasks; it's about fundamentally rethinking how supply chains are managed, optimized, and leveraged for strategic advantage.

AI technologies have introduced a level of intelligence in supply chain operations that was once unimaginable. By integrating AI, businesses can now foresee and respond to the complexities of supply and demand with unprecedented accuracy. Machine learning algorithms, for instance, analyze historical data to predict demand patterns, helping companies to align their inventory strategies accordingly. This predictive capability minimizes overstocking and stockouts, ensuring a balanced inventory that meets customer needs without incurring excessive costs.

Moreover, the power of AI in enhancing supply chain efficiency is not limited to demand forecasting. One of the compelling applications is in logistics and transportation. AI-driven platforms optimize delivery routes and modes, reducing transit times and fuel consumption. These platforms can adapt in real-time, rerouting shipments based on traffic conditions, weather patterns, or unexpected delays, thereby improving delivery reliability and reducing transportation costs.

The significance of AI extends beyond logistics optimization to include warehouse management. Through computer vision and robotics, AI streamlines warehouse operations, from sorting and picking to packing and dispatching. This automation reduces human error and accelerates the fulfillment process, allowing businesses to scale their operations in response to increasing demand while maintaining a high level of accuracy and efficiency.

Supplier relationship management is another area where AI makes a considerable impact. By harnessing natural language processing and advanced analytics, companies can monitor supplier performance, manage risks, and ensure compliance. AI tools offer insights into potential disruptions, enabling proactive measures that prevent supply chain interruptions. Enhanced visibility across the supply chain fosters stronger partnerships and supports strategic decision-making in supplier management.

Let's not overlook the role of AI in sustainability, an increasingly critical concern in supply chain management. AI helps identify inefficiencies and areas of waste throughout the supply chain, providing recommendations for more sustainable practices. By optimizing resource usage and minimizing environmental impact, businesses not only improve their sustainability profiles but also gain competitive advantages in markets that value corporate responsibility.

Empowering supply chain professionals with AI-driven tools also facilitates better risk management. The complexity and interconnectedness of modern supply chains make them vulnerable to a myriad of risks, from geopolitical instability to natural disasters. AI systems enhance risk assessment by simulating various scenarios, predicting potential disruptions, and suggesting mitigation strategies. This proactive approach to risk management is crucial for maintaining continuity and resilience in supply chain operations.

Adopting AI for supply chain efficiency isn't without challenges, however. Creating a truly intelligent supply chain demands a foundational shift in how data is managed. The integration of systems and the sharing of data across platforms can be challenging, requiring careful strategy and alignment with business goals. Moreover, developing the necessary AI competencies within teams is essential to fully leverage these technologies and foster a culture of continuous improvement and innovation.

In conclusion, the enhancement of supply chain efficiency through AI is not just a technological advancement; it is a strategic imperative for modern businesses. By optimizing operations, reducing costs, and improving service levels, AI in the supply chain creates value that reverberates throughout the organization. The pursuit of AI-driven supply chain efficiency embodies a forward-thinking approach to operations management, positioning companies to meet future challenges and opportunities with agility and precision.

Chapter 9:
AI in Financial Decision Making

In the dynamic realm of finance, the integration of AI has become a game-changer, equipping business leaders with tools to refine decision-making processes with unprecedented precision. AI's capacity to process vast datasets allows organizations to conduct comprehensive risk assessments, leading to more informed and timely financial decisions. By leveraging AI-driven insights, businesses can enhance their investment strategies, identifying lucrative opportunities while mitigating potential pitfalls. The analytical prowess of AI not only elevates efficiency and accuracy but also frees financial professionals from routine data analysis, enabling them to focus on strategic planning and innovation. As AI continues to evolve, its transformative impact on financial decision-making will only grow, presenting forward-thinking companies with the chance to redefine competitive advantage in a rapidly changing market landscape.

Risk Assessment with AI

In the fast-paced world of finance, risk lurks at every corner. From market volatility to credit defaults, financial institutions constantly navigate an ocean of uncertainty. Enter Artificial Intelligence (AI), a beacon of hope in this sea of potential hazards. The integration of AI into risk assessment processes is transforming the way financial decisions are made, offering precision, speed, and insightful strategies that were once out of reach.

AI systems have revolutionized risk assessment by enhancing the ability to predict and manage financial risks effectively. These systems process vast amounts of data at an unprecedented speed, identifying patterns and potential threats that are imperceptible to the human eye. What this means for financial professionals is a paradigm shift—from reactive measures to proactive risk management approaches, as AI can forecast potential problems before they materialize.

One of the core advantages of AI in risk assessment is its capability to provide accurate credit scoring. Traditional credit assessment models, while still valuable, are often limited by their reliance on historical data and traditional metrics. AI comes equipped with machine learning algorithms capable of evaluating a broader set of variables, including non-traditional data points like social media usage, online behavior, and other digital footprints. This holistic view not only augments the accuracy of credit scoring but also expands access to financial services for individuals who might be assessed as higher-risk by conventional methods.

The predictive power of AI is another transformational quality. Machine learning algorithms can analyze data from financial markets to predict stock movements, interest rate changes, and potential economic downturns. This forecasting ability is invaluable, allowing financial institutions to adjust their portfolios and strategies accordingly, minimizing exposure to risk. In this fast-evolving environment, businesses harness AI to enhance their risk-adjusted returns, aligning their financial maneuvers with predictive analytics.

However, the deployment of AI in financial risk assessment is not without its challenges. The black-box nature of some AI models can lead to issues with transparency and explainability. Understanding how AI reaches its conclusions is crucial; otherwise, stakeholders might find it challenging to fully trust these systems. Financial institutions must ensure that their AI models are auditable and interpretable, promoting confidence among users and regulators alike. Here, emerging efforts in developing explainable AI (XAI) become pivotal, aiming to shed light on the decision-making processes of AI systems.

Another significant aspect to consider is data security and privacy. In finance, where customer data is both valuable and highly sensitive, maintaining stringent data protection standards is non-negotiable. AI systems necessitate large datasets to function effectively, which raises potential concerns over data breaches and unauthorized access. Financial institutions must invest in robust cybersecurity measures to safeguard this information, ensuring compliance with evolving data protection regulations like the General Data Protection Regulation (GDPR) and the California Consumer Privacy Act (CCPA).

Moreover, ethical considerations should not be sidelined. Bias in AI algorithms is a critical concern that can lead to unfair outcomes, particularly in credit lending and insurance underwriting. AI systems reflect the data they are trained on, and if that data carries biases, so too will the AI's assessments. Implementing rigorous bias detection and mitigation strategies is necessary to ensure fairness and equality in financial decision-making processes. Institutions need to test biases not just within their AI models, but throughout their data pipelines, continuously refining and validating inputs and outputs.

Despite these challenges, the benefits AI brings to risk assessment are substantial, and with proper management, they far outweigh the concerns. By embracing these technologies, financial institutions can enhance their resilience against future crises, ensuring a more stable economic landscape. The strategic use of AI in finance requires not just technological adoption but also a cultural shift within organizations, promoting an AI-aware workforce that is skilled in interpreting and utilizing their findings effectively.

In conclusion, AI's role in risk assessment is transformative, promising to bring about significant improvements in the precision and agility of financial decision-making. As financial leaders and organizations continue to adapt, the ability to leverage AI for risk assessment stands as a competitive advantage. This new wave of technological advancement is not merely about efficiency or profitability—it's about sustainability and informed decision-making in an increasingly complex financial ecosystem. Through careful application and continuous refinement, AI will continue to reshape the landscape of financial risk assessment, offering unprecedented insight into one of the most critical aspects of the industry.

Improving Investment Strategies

In today's fast-paced financial landscape, leveraging AI in investment strategies can significantly enhance decision-making capabilities. By harnessing advanced algorithms and data processing, businesses can refine their investment approaches to be more predictive, data-driven, and responsive to market changes. With AI, investors can analyze vast data sets that were previously too complex or time-consuming for human analysis, extracting insights that drive better investment decisions.

The ability to predict market movements and trends is crucial for any investor. AI systems can assimilate historical market data, identifying patterns and anomalies that might be easy to overlook with traditional analysis. These insights enable investors to anticipate shifts in the market, reacting swiftly to potential risks and opportunities. Machine learning algorithms, for instance, can process financial news, social media sentiment, and global events to forecast market behavior, allowing investors to make informed decisions with a higher degree of confidence.

Moreover, AI systems excel in risk management, an integral part of crafting successful investment strategies. By evaluating both qualitative and quantitative data, AI solutions can assess the potential risks associated with each investment, offering a clearer picture of the possible outcomes and helping investors allocate resources efficiently. This isn't just about avoiding potential loss; it's about strategically positioning investments to maximize returns with a well-balanced approach.

Portfolio optimization is another area where AI makes a significant impact. By continuously analyzing and learning from market data, AI can recommend optimal asset allocations that align with an investor's risk tolerance and financial goals. The dynamic nature of these algorithms ensures that the portfolio is always aligned with current market conditions, providing a competitive edge that manual methods simply can't match.

Additionally, AI-driven investment strategies can contribute to sustainability goals, an increasingly important consideration for modern investors. By incorporating environmental, social, and governance (ESG) criteria into their analysis, AI systems can help identify companies that not only promise financial returns but also adhere to sustainable practices. This dual focus supports both ethical investing and long-term financial success, creating a win-win situation for investors seeking to make a positive impact.

Another exciting development is the real-time data analysis capability offered by AI. Traditionally, investors have relied on end-of-day reports to make decisions. In contrast, AI can provide real-time data analytics, empowering investors to act instantly on market events as they happen. This immediacy allows for more agile responses, adjusting strategies in real time to capitalize on fleeting opportunities or mitigate unexpected risks.

The integration of AI in investment strategies also democratizes access to sophisticated analytical tools. Previously, only large financial institutions could afford to implement complex data analysis and prediction models. With AI, however, smaller firms and individual investors can now leverage the same caliber of tools, leveling the playing field and broadening the scope for informed investment decisions.

Moreover, AI not only enhances decision-making but also promotes greater transparency. AI systems can track and explain the rationale behind particular investment recommendations, offering insights into the decision-making process. This transparency is crucial for building trust with clients and stakeholders, who are increasingly seeking assurance on the methods behind financial decisions.

Implementing AI in investment strategies doesn't come without challenges, though. There's a steep learning curve when adapting to AI's data-centricity. Financial professionals must be prepared to evolve their skills, understanding the tools and technologies driving AI. This includes collaborating with data scientists and AI experts to build strategies that best utilize these advanced systems.

However, the rewards are well worth the effort. The competitive edge gained through AI-driven strategies positions businesses to navigate the financial markets with greater agility and insight. Future-proofing investment strategies by incorporating AI technologies ensures that businesses remain resilient amid economic shifts and evolving market dynamics.

As we move forward, the synergy between human intuition and AI capabilities will redefine investment strategies. While AI handles data processing and pattern recognition, human investors bring the contextual understanding and emotional intelligence necessary for nuanced decision-making. This collaboration between human and machine fosters a comprehensive approach to investment, uniting analytical power with strategic acumen.

In conclusion, while the journey towards integrating AI into investment strategies demands change and adaptation, the potential benefits are transformative. Businesses that embrace this technological shift stand to not only increase their financial returns but also enhance their strategic positioning within the market. AI is not just another tool in the investor's toolkit; it's an evolution in the way investment strategies are crafted and executed, heralding a new era of informed, strategic, and sustainable investing.

Chapter 10:
AI in Human Resources

As organizations navigate the digital transformation, AI is proving to be a game-changer in the realm of human resources. By leveraging AI, companies can revolutionize talent acquisition, streamline recruitment processes, and enhance employee retention strategies, ensuring they attract and keep top talent in an increasingly competitive market. AI-driven platforms are now adept at analyzing vast amounts of data to identify the most suitable candidates and predict employee success, drastically reducing time and resources spent on traditional methods. Furthermore, AI tools are reshaping performance evaluations by providing objective insights and personalized feedback, fostering a more dynamic and productive workplace environment. This automation not only elevates the efficiency of HR departments but also crafts a more engaging and supportive ecosystem for employees, empowering organizations to stay agile and responsive to workforce needs.

Talent Acquisition and Retention

The modern business landscape is ever-evolving, with technological advancements leading the charge. As the pace quickens, the cornerstone of any successful organization remains its people. Talent acquisition and retention, therefore, not only reflect an organization's strategic priorities but also its capabilities to adapt and thrive. Emerging technologies, particularly Artificial Intelligence (AI), are redefining how businesses approach these crucial facets of human resources.

At the heart of talent acquisition, AI offers a profound shift in identifying, engaging, and securing top talent. AI-driven systems are adept at parsing through vast quantities of data, providing HR professionals with insights that were previously unattainable. For example, AI algorithms can traverse candidates' resumes, analyze social media activity, and evaluate professional networks to create a comprehensive profile. This isn't just about efficiency but precision—ensuring the right talent is identified, and the hiring process is streamlined.

But AI's role doesn't stop there. It's also pivotal in enhancing candidate experience. By utilizing chatbots and virtual assistants, companies can ensure timely communication and immediate responses to potential candidates, thereby improving engagement. These AI tools can guide applicants through the recruitment process, answer queries, and keep them informed, significantly reducing drop-off rates.

Moreover, AI empowers recruiters to eliminate human biases, consciously or unconsciously present, during the hiring process. Traditional recruitment methods may inadvertently favor certain demographics or backgrounds, but AI-based solutions provide uniform criteria, aligning the selection process more closely with the job requirements. By training AI models on diverse datasets, organizations can ensure a fair and equitable evaluation, promoting a diverse and inclusive workforce.

Importantly, talent retention goes hand-in-hand with acquisition. Where AI in acquisition focuses on sourcing and bringing in new talent, AI in retention emphasizes keeping employees engaged, motivated, and satisfied in their roles. Employee disengagement is a silent yet pervasive issue that AI can help tackle. Predictive analytics, a key component of AI, can identify potential churn risks by gauging employee sentiment through emails, surveys, and other communications. By understanding these indicators early, HR can intervene with tailored retention strategies.

Engagement platforms powered by AI can provide real-time feedback loops, allowing employees to voice their concerns and aspirations continuously. Understanding team dynamics and individual preferences through data analysis, managers can implement personalized career development plans and offer targeted training opportunities. Such proactive measures not only enhance job satisfaction but also align individual growth with organizational goals.

Additionally, AI facilitates a culture of learning and development beyond traditional methods. Adaptive learning platforms can assess an employee's current skills and recommend personalized learning paths, fostering continuous professional growth. These platforms analyze learning patterns, ensuring that employees receive content most relevant to their career trajectory, facilitating sustained engagement.

The integration of AI in talent acquisition and retention strategies is ultimately a testament to a company's commitment to innovation and its workforce. However, the technology is not without challenges. Data privacy concerns are legitimate, as handling personal and sensitive employee data requires strict adherence to ethical guidelines and legal regulations. Organizations must be transparent about how data is used, ensuring it is safeguarded and managed with respect and integrity.

The transformation AI brings to the HR domain doesn't exist in isolation. It needs a strategic framework aligning with broader organizational objectives. For business leaders aiming to deploy AI-driven HR solutions, it's essential to foster a culture that embraces change and continuous learning. Training HR personnel to effectively use AI tools will also be vital to maximizing their potential and driving sustained organizational growth.

In conclusion, AI's potential to revolutionize talent acquisition and retention is substantial. By adopting AI intelligently, businesses can enhance recruitment efficiency, ensure equity, and promote employee satisfaction and growth. As we continue into an AI-accelerated future, embracing these technologies will remain crucial for companies dedicated to maintaining a competitive edge and nurturing a thriving workforce.

AI for Employee Performance Evaluation

Artificial Intelligence (AI) has incessantly advanced to a point where it's transforming various facets of business operations, and human resources (HR) is no exception. Among its significant contributions to HR, AI ushered in a new era for employee performance evaluation. This segment not only simplifies the evaluation process but also adds layers of objectivity and comprehensiveness that were previously challenging to achieve. A traditional performance review might rely heavily on subjective assessments, whereas AI leverages vast amounts of data to map out a clearer, unbiased picture of an employee's performance.

At the core of AI-driven performance evaluation is data. It's data that powers AI's ability to comprehend, analyze, and forecast performance trends. Historically, the data might have included basic metrics like attendance or sales figures. However, AI can now integrate diverse data sources, from productivity tool usage to communication patterns, providing a multi-dimensional view of an employee's contribution to the organization. The integration of such data enables HR professionals to pinpoint strengths and areas for improvement with greater accuracy than ever before.

As businesses continue to embrace remote and hybrid work environments, AI becomes even more crucial. Virtual work settings can obscure some of the behavioral cues that managers depend on for performance assessment. With AI, companies are equipped to analyze work output without the geographical limitations previously posed. Patterns in employee interactions, digital presence, and delivery of work can be accurately gauged, offering a realistic evaluation of performance without the constraints of physical presence.

Moreover, AI's proactive nature can't be overstated. Instead of waiting for annual or semi-annual reviews, AI systems can continuously monitor performance, providing real-time feedback to employees. This immediate feedback loop not only helps in rectifying issues as they appear but also in recognizing and rewarding high performance promptly. In effect, AI helps in cultivating a culture of continuous improvement and recognition.

Adopting AI in performance evaluations doesn't mean replacing the human element. On the contrary, it augments the human touch by providing managers with substantial insights to facilitate more meaningful discussions. Managers can spend less time on data gathering and more time on coaching, mentorship, and personal development, which ultimately unlocks higher employee potential.

One of the key challenges, however, lies in ensuring transparency and understanding. Employees might harbor concerns about being monitored or evaluated by machines, perceived as impersonal or invasive. It is essential for organizations to ensure that AI tools and techniques they wield are transparent and customers know how decisions are made and what data is being used. Consequently, building trust is paramount, requiring open communication and ethical handling of data.

Skilled HR leaders will navigate these nuances by blending AI insights with empathetic leadership. They will translate AI-generated data into narratives that employees can relate to and use for their personal growth. AI should be seen as an ally, streamlining administrative tasks and offering powerful insights that foster a thriving organizational culture. It becomes the manager's compass, guiding decisions while acknowledging the unique human experiences that each employee brings to the table.

The shift towards AI-enhanced performance evaluation necessitates redefining performance indicators. Traditional metrics may not fully encapsulate the essence of an employee's role or potential. By using AI to uncover hidden patterns and predictors of success, businesses can redefine KPIs to align with a dynamic work environment. This redefinition is crucial for maintaining competitiveness and ensuring that performance reviews are truly reflective of contribution and potential.

Moreover, AI-engines can benchmark performance against industry standards. This benchmarking process not only illuminates where an organization stands but also identifies opportunities for employees to elevate their competencies. Such strategic insights are invaluable for both organization and employee growth.

As AI technology continues to evolve, it's important for business leaders to remain adaptable, continually learning and integrating new tools into their HR practices. These leaders must also focus on upskilling and reskilling their workforce, equipping employees to harness AI-driven insights for self-improvement. Investment in training and development ensures that both managers and employees are comfortable interpreting and benefiting from AI insights.

In conclusion, leveraging AI in employee performance evaluation is not merely about technology adoption but about spearheading a cultural shift towards data-driven decision-making within HR. Through thoughtful implementation and leadership, AI can significantly enhance employee performance evaluation, leading to a more engaged, satisfied, and high-performing workforce. As businesses navigate this transformative journey, they'll not only optimize the evaluation process but also better align employee performance with business objectives, ultimately driving organizational success.

Chapter 11:
Ethical Considerations in AI

As businesses increasingly turn to artificial intelligence to drive decision-making and gain a competitive edge, they face profound ethical considerations that can't be ignored. The deployment of AI systems brings to light issues such as bias, which can inadvertently perpetuate inequality if not carefully managed. It's crucial for organizations to design AI with fairness in mind, ensuring that systems are scrutinized for unintended prejudices. Alongside this, safeguarding privacy is paramount—customers and stakeholders expect their data to be handled with utmost care, and breaches could have not only legal ramifications but also damage trust. Business leaders must lead by example, embedding ethical AI practices into their corporate cultures and operational strategies. By championing transparency and accountability, they not only protect their enterprises but also contribute to a more ethical tech landscape, where innovation serves the greater good without compromising individual rights. Navigating these challenges requires vigilant attention and a commitment to principles that balance progress with responsibility.

Addressing Bias in AI Systems

As artificial intelligence (AI) becomes a cornerstone of strategic decision-making for businesses, understanding and addressing bias in AI systems is not just an ethical responsibility; it's a critical business imperative. Bias, if left unchecked, can lead to flawed decisions that not only tarnish a company's reputation but also lead to financial loss and legal challenges. The power of AI lies in its ability to analyze vast amounts of data and make decisions that humans might find challenging to comprehend. However, this very capability can be compromised by bias, resulting in outcomes that reinforce stereotypes or marginalize groups.

Bias in AI can enter the system at various stages. From the initial data collection process to algorithm development and deployment, each phase presents opportunities for biases to slip in. Data, being the lifeblood of AI, carries the historical and societal biases that exist in the real world. Inadvertent biases in the data, if not identified and corrected, can cascade through the AI model, leading to prejudiced decision-making. Business leaders must ensure that the data used is diverse, representative, and free from historical prejudices. This requires a conscious effort in curating data datasets that reflect fairness and equality.

Algorithmic bias, another critical facet, occurs when the algorithms themselves are structured in a manner that results in unjust outcomes. This can be due to the unintentional design of biased decision rules or the inadequacy of the model to interpret data without prejudice. It's vital for developers and data scientists to scrutinize their algorithms, testing them rigorously against a diverse array of situations and outcomes. Only by doing so can they ensure that AI systems make equitable decisions that respect the diversity of global consumer bases.

Transparent AI systems are crucial for mitigating bias. Industries must push for transparency where the development and decision-making processes of AI are publicly accessible for evaluation. This transparency fosters trust among users and stakeholders while providing opportunities for continuous improvement. Ethically developed AI communicates its decision-making rationale in an understandable manner, allowing human oversight to explain and rectify potential biases.

Moreover, establishing an AI ethics committee or task force within organizations can provide an ongoing review of AI systems' decisions and impact. These committees, ideally comprising diverse and interdisciplinary teams, can provide the checks and balances necessary to evaluate AI biases systematically. Regular audits performed by these committees ensure that AI systems evolve with changing societal norms and values while maintaining adherence to ethical guidelines.

Education and awareness play a significant role in addressing bias. Business leaders should prioritize upskilling teams on recognizing and mitigating biases in AI. This doesn't only apply to data scientists and developers but extends to all employees engaged in AI-dependent activities. Insight into the operations of AI systems helps individuals identify bias and advocate for fairness in AI-driven processes. As employees become more knowledgeable about AI's potential pitfalls, they become proactive partners in fostering ethical AI practices within an organization.

Another powerful method for addressing AI bias is through collaborative efforts across industries. By sharing insights, tools, and best practices, organizations can collectively advance the mitigation of bias. Pioneering companies can lead by example, showcasing their strategies and successes in creating fair and inclusive AI systems. This collaboration plays a pivotal role in setting industry standards and creating a unified approach to ethical AI deployment.

Incentivizing fairness in AI is also crucial for industry-wide change. Regulatory bodies and industry standards should promote practices fostering unbiased AI development. Incentives, such as certifications for bias-free AI systems, could motivate organizations to meet high ethical standards. These certifications not only provide a competitive advantage but also signal to consumers that a company is committed to fairness and equality.

In conclusion, addressing bias in AI systems is indispensable not just for ethical reasons but for ensuring business efficacy and success. Decision-makers must remain vigilant and proactive in identifying and mitigating biases throughout AI's lifecycle. Organizations that master the art of unbiased AI will ultimately gain not only a moral edge but also a competitive advantage by winning the trust of their customers and stakeholders alike. The road to bias-free AI is complex, but with deliberate strategies and continuous improvement, businesses can harness AI's potential responsibly and ethically.

Ensuring Privacy and Security

In the rapidly evolving landscape of artificial intelligence, ensuring privacy and security has become one of the most pressing ethical considerations. As business leaders and decision-makers begin integrating AI systems into their strategic frameworks, the importance of safeguarding sensitive data cannot be overstated. AI systems rely heavily on vast amounts of data, and this dependency places a significant responsibility on businesses to protect the privacy of individuals whose data is at stake.

Today, privacy concerns have reached unprecedented levels. The more AI systems rely on personal data to generate insights and predictions, the higher the stakes in maintaining confidentiality. In a time where data breaches and cyber threats are commonplace, businesses can't afford to fall short in implementing rigorous security protocols. Strong security measures are not just a legal obligation but a moral one, fostering trust among consumers and business partners.

The challenge lies in balancing the immense capabilities of AI with the ethical obligation to protect individual privacy. As powerful as AI can be in transforming business processes, this power must be wielded responsibly. AI systems often analyze, process, and store vast amounts of personally identifiable information (PII). If this data is not adequately protected, it could lead to severe privacy violations with long-lasting repercussions.

One effective strategy to ensure privacy is data anonymization. This process involves stripping data of identifiable characteristics, thus permitting its use for AI training and analysis without compromising individual privacy. However, businesses must tread carefully, as not all anonymization techniques provide foolproof protection. Continuous advancements in re-identification methods challenge data anonymization, necessitating constant vigilance and adaptation.

Moreover, AI systems must be designed with privacy in mind from the ground up. This concept, often referred to as "privacy by design," involves incorporating privacy measures during the development stage rather than as an afterthought. By embedding privacy features into the AI development lifecycle, businesses can mitigate risks more effectively. Privacy by design encourages proactive thinking and long-term strategy in the realm of data protection.

In addition to privacy, security is a crucial component of ethical AI deployment. An AI system is only as secure as its weakest link. Cybersecurity threats can compromise not only the data but also the functionality of AI systems, leading to potential misinformation and erratic outputs. Implementing robust encryption protocols and access controls are foundational steps toward securing AI systems against unauthorized access and cyberattacks.

Furthermore, it's essential for organizations to foster a culture of data security and privacy awareness. Employees at all levels should be educated about the significance of protecting sensitive information and the potential repercussions of security breaches. Regular training sessions and workshops can help update teams on the latest security protocols and best practices. Such initiatives cultivate a security-centric mindset, making it a shared responsibility rather than an isolated IT function.

It's also worth noting that privacy and security considerations extend beyond the technical aspects. Legal and regulatory frameworks, such as the General Data Protection Regulation (GDPR) in Europe, set the boundaries for data use and protection. Compliance with such regulations is not optional; it's mandatory. Non-compliance can lead to hefty fines and irreparable damage to an organization's reputation. Hence, businesses must stay informed about evolving regulations and adjust their practices accordingly.

Another key element is transparency in AI operations. Businesses should be transparent about how they collect, use, and store data. This transparency builds trust with customers who are increasingly concerned about how their personal information is being used. Providing clear and understandable privacy policies and obtaining explicit consent for data use are vital steps in this direction. Transparency doesn't just prevent potential ethical breaches, it also enhances the company's credibility and customer loyalty.

Finally, collaboration and sharing of best practices across industries can significantly enhance privacy and security standards. Businesses should engage in open dialogues with partners, stakeholders, and even competitors to share knowledge and strategies on securing AI systems. Collective efforts in standardizing security practices can drive industry-wide improvements, creating a safer digital environment for everyone involved.

In conclusion, ensuring privacy and security in AI is a multifaceted challenge, yet one that is essential for trustworthy and ethical AI adoption. Business professionals, as the custodians of sensitive data, have an imperative role in shaping policies and systems that prioritize privacy and security. By fostering a culture of vigilance and transparency, embracing technological advancements, and adhering to regulatory mandates, businesses can confidently embrace AI's transformative potential while safeguarding the trust placed in them by their stakeholders.

Chapter 12:
AI Implementation Challenges

Navigating the landscape of AI implementation presents a unique set of challenges for businesses eager to harness its transformative power. While the potential rewards are significant, integrating AI into existing systems requires both strategic foresight and practical agility. Companies often face resistance to change, as teams grapple with altered workflows and fear of job displacement. Additionally, the complexity of AI technologies demands specialized skills that may not be readily available, necessitating investment in training and development. Overcoming these barriers requires a dual focus: fostering an adaptable corporate culture and ensuring robust change management processes. Moreover, successful AI adoption hinges on clear alignment with organizational goals, promoting collaboration across departments, and sustaining long-term commitment from leadership. By addressing these challenges head-on, organizations can position themselves not only to incorporate AI effectively but to thrive in an increasingly automated world.

Overcoming Barriers to AI Adoption

Implementing Artificial Intelligence in any organization is not without its challenges. Yet, the roadblocks to adopting AI can be seen not as insurmountable, but as opportunities for growth and innovation. Companies that navigate these challenges successfully often emerge stronger and more competitive. Understanding these barriers and developing strategies to overcome them is essential for future-proofing businesses in an increasingly AI-driven world.

One of the most significant barriers to AI adoption is the lack of understanding about what AI can truly accomplish. Business leaders might be enthusiastic about the potential of AI but lack a clear roadmap of how to integrate it into their strategic plans. The fear of the unknown can be debilitating. This anxiety often stems from misconceptions about AI capabilities, leading to inflated expectations or unwarranted fears. Educating stakeholders about realistic AI applications tailored to specific business goals is crucial. Empowering decision-makers with knowledge dispels myths and opens the door to pragmatic AI strategies that align with enterprise objectives.

An organization's cultural readiness is another critical factor affecting AI adoption. Resistance to change is a natural human instinct; it's no different when it comes to technology. Employees may fear that AI will replace them, undermining their roles and job security. To counter this perception, companies must invest in creating a culture that sees AI as a collaborative partner rather than a threat. This includes transparent communication about AI's role and benefits, along with involving employees in the AI integration process. By fostering a culture that values learning and innovation, businesses can turn potential skepticism into enthusiasm.

Data is often touted as the new oil, yet many companies struggle with data management challenges. Issues around data quality, accessibility, and integration can stifle AI initiatives before they even begin. High-quality data is a prerequisite for successful AI models; without it, outputs can be unreliable. Organizations should prioritize establishing robust data governance frameworks that ensure data accuracy, security, and relevance. Additionally, fostering collaboration between IT and business units can streamline data flow and accessibility, creating a unified data strategy that supports AI initiatives.

The technical skills gap presents yet another hurdle. AI technologies evolve rapidly, requiring a workforce that is skilled in the latest tools and methodologies. However, there is a widespread shortage of professionals with the requisite AI expertise. To fill this gap, organizations must invest in upskilling and reskilling their workforce. Partnering with educational institutions for tailored AI courses or encouraging continuous learning through online platforms can help bridge this gap. Additionally, integrating AI experts into teams ensures that knowledge is distributed, fostering an environment where technical know-how is shared and leveraged across the organization.

Financial constraints also play a significant role in impeding AI adoption. The costs associated with AI initiatives can be significant, encompassing investments in technology, infrastructure, and talent. Smaller businesses, in particular, may view these costs as prohibitive. However, creative solutions can mitigate financial barriers. Progressive companies explore options like incremental implementation, starting with pilot projects that demonstrate measurable benefits before scaling. Partnerships and collaborations with AI technology vendors can also provide access to tools at reduced costs, allowing businesses to experiment without heavy upfront investments.

In parallel, the complexity of AI systems can intimidate businesses from wholeheartedly committing to their adoption. These systems often require sophisticated infrastructures and continuous monitoring to ensure optimal performance. Simplifying AI adoption through the use of accessible, user-friendly platforms can alleviate these concerns. As cloud-based AI solutions gain traction, they provide scalable options for businesses to experiment with AI without the need for extensive technical infrastructure.

Addressing regulatory and ethical concerns is another area where businesses must tread carefully. As AI systems become pervasive, they intersect with areas related to data privacy, security, and ethical use. Businesses need to align their AI strategies with existing regulations to avoid legal pitfalls. Proactively addressing these concerns not only safeguards the company but also builds trust with customers and stakeholders. Establishing ethical guidelines and compliance measures within AI projects can serve as a proactive approach, demonstrating a commitment to ethical AI practices.

Strategic leadership plays an instrumental role in overcoming barriers to AI adoption. Leadership needs to articulate a clear vision for AI integration, ensuring that it ties into broader business strategies and outcomes. Visionary leaders embrace AI's potential while pragmatically addressing the associated challenges. They understand that fostering an innovation-centric culture is crucial to sustaining AI growth and integration. By championing AI initiatives, prioritizing investment in necessary resources, and setting quantifiable goals, leaders can set the tone for successful AI adoption.

Additionally, understanding customer demands and market forces can provide companies with insights into how best to leverage AI. In an age where customer experiences drive success, harnessing AI to personalize interactions and tailor offerings can be a game-changer. AI opens up new avenues for understanding market trends and consumer behavior, but only if companies are willing to adapt and innovate in line with these insights.

Ultimately, the journey to AI adoption is marked with obstacles, but these can be transformed into stepping stones. Companies that are open to learning, that work to align AI with their strategic goals, and invest in the necessary resources and culture, will find success. Overcoming these barriers not only paves the way for ample ROI but also places organizations at the frontline of innovation, ready to seize opportunities in the ever-evolving digital landscape.

Managing Change in AI Projects

Change management is a cornerstone of successful AI project implementation. In today's rapidly evolving business landscape, AI projects introduce not just new technology, but a new way of thinking. They demand shifts in processes, employee roles, and organizational culture. Leaders must guide their companies through these changes with vision and clarity, ensuring that AI initiatives align with overarching business goals and result in tangible improvements.

One of the first steps in managing change is fostering an environment that embraces AI. This begins at the top. Executive leadership should clearly articulate the value AI brings and the strategic objectives it serves. Transparency is crucial here—staff should understand why AI is being implemented and the benefits it can offer. Open communication can alleviate fears of job displacement and build trust, which is essential for successful technological integration.

Another critical aspect is involving employees in the process. Rather than imposing change from above, engage teams at all levels. Encourage participation in identifying potential AI applications and involve key personnel in pilot projects. This not only utilizes existing expertise within the organization but also empowers employees, fostering a sense of ownership and commitment to the project's success.

Training and education are indispensable in managing change effectively. AI's complexity can be daunting, and misconceptions abound. Investing in comprehensive training programs demystifies the technology, equipping staff with the knowledge they need to work alongside AI solutions. Such initiatives should include both technical skills and broader understanding of AI's potential impact on business models.

Resistance is inevitable in any change process, and AI projects are no exception. Leaders need to be prepared to meet opposition with empathy rather than confrontation. Take the time to understand concerns and provide tailored solutions to address them. Sometimes, the resistance stems from a lack of understanding about how AI will benefit specific roles. Demonstrating how AI can augment human skills rather than replace them can significantly reduce apprehension.

Creating a feedback loop is an effective strategy to manage change. Regularly solicit feedback from employees at all stages of AI implementation. Doing so not only identifies pain points and areas for improvement but also engages staff in ongoing development. When employees see their input leading to tangible changes, it reinforces their investment in the project's success.

Adaptability and flexibility must be at the core of managing change in AI projects. The dynamism inherent in AI means that projects can quickly pivot from their initial trajectory. Leaders should encourage a culture that's open to iterative learning and agile responses. This adaptive approach not only benefits the current AI project but also ingrains a mindset that's invaluable in future technological evolutions.

Performance metrics play a vital role in managing change, providing benchmarks for success and areas needing adjustment. It's crucial to establish clear, measurable objectives that align with business goals. This allows for the evaluation of AI's return on investment and demonstrates its effectiveness to stakeholders. When AI projects visibly contribute to business achievements, it entrenches their necessity within the organization.

Moreover, managing change in AI projects requires an acute awareness of the broader ethical and social implications. Businesses that integrate AI must do so responsibly, addressing issues of bias, privacy, and transparency. This not only aligns with ethical practices but also mitigates potential reputational risks, ensuring that AI initiatives are sustainable in the long term.

In conclusion, effective change management in AI projects is multifaceted, encompassing leadership, employee engagement, continuous learning, and ethical considerations. It's not merely about adopting new technology—it's about evolving organizational culture to thrive alongside it. Business leaders who navigate these waters successfully will find AI not only transforms their operations but also elevates their competitive stance in the market.

Chapter 13:
Leadership and AI Competence

In the rapidly evolving landscape of AI integration, effective leadership is paramount to navigating the transformative shift towards intelligent technology. Business leaders today are tasked with developing AI competencies not only within themselves but also within their teams to harness AI's potential effectively. A nuanced understanding of AI capabilities and limitations allows leaders to identify opportunities where AI can drive value and enhance decision-making. It requires fostering a culture that is data-driven, where insights are used strategically to guide innovation and efficiency. Achieving AI competence involves a commitment to continuous learning and adaptation, encouraging teams to embrace change and develop a forward-thinking approach. Leaders must cultivate an environment where openness to experimentation with AI tools and technologies thrives, merging strategic vision with technological acumen to maintain a competitive edge. This blend of skills and mindset ensures that organizations remain agile and poised for future advancements in the AI domain, empowering teams to undertake bold strategies that lead to sustainable success.

Developing AI Competencies in Teams

In the rapidly evolving landscape of artificial intelligence (AI), the need for teams to develop AI competencies has never been more pressing. Organizations looking to maintain a competitive edge are increasingly relying on AI to drive strategic decision-making and improve operational efficiency. But leveraging AI is not just about adopting technology—it's about ensuring that human talent is equipped with the necessary skills and mindset to harness AI's potential.

Building AI competencies within teams starts with a fundamental shift in how we view education and professional development. Traditional learning paradigms often focus on specific technical skills. While these are important, AI requires a more holistic approach that spans technical, analytical, and even philosophical domains. It's not just about understanding algorithms or data science—it's about grasping how AI can transform a business process or solve a complex problem.

The first step in this journey is creating a culture of continuous learning. Teams should be encouraged to stay curious, explore new advancements, and frequently upskill. This is where leadership plays a crucial role. Leaders must advocate for continuous professional development and provide the necessary resources, such as access to online courses, workshops, and seminars focused on AI technologies and their applications in business.

Moreover, fostering AI competencies also involves breaking down silos within an organization. AI development is inherently interdisciplinary; it flourishes at the intersection of different skills and perspectives. Encouraging cross-functional collaboration allows diverse teams to contribute their unique insights, leading to more innovative AI applications. Cross-department projects can bridge the gap between data scientists, IT professionals, domain experts, and business leaders, ensuring a well-rounded approach to AI development.

An essential aspect of developing AI competencies is promoting a mindset ready for change. Teams should be adaptable and open to experimentation and failure. AI projects often involve trial and error, necessitating a culture where failure is seen as a stepping stone to success rather than an endpoint. This mindset encourages learning from mistakes and drives iterative improvements in AI implementations.

Technical skills, while not the only requirement, are undeniably a significant component of AI competence. Organizations should identify the skills most relevant to their specific AI goals—whether that's machine learning, deep learning, natural language processing, or another sub-domain. Tailored training programs should then be developed to cater to these needs, incorporating practical, hands-on experiences alongside theoretical knowledge.

In line with technical skills, data literacy should be a primary focus of team development. Data is the lifeblood of AI, and understanding how to collect, analyze, and interpret data is critical. Teams should be proficient in managing data sources, ensuring its quality, and transforming it into actionable insights. This competence is essential for making informed decisions that drive AI strategies forward.

On the softer side of skills, critical thinking and problem-solving are invaluable. AI thrives on clear objectives and precise questions. Hence, cultivating the ability to analyze problems from multiple angles and frame questions in a way that AI systems can address effectively is crucial. This involves understanding the limitations of AI and developing strategies that leverage its strengths while mitigating its weaknesses.

Communication skills also play a pivotal role. The ability to articulate AI-related insights to non-technical stakeholders is essential for ensuring the broader organization understands and buys into AI initiatives. This communication helps in aligning AI projects with broader business outcomes and facilitates smoother adoption of AI-driven solutions.

Developing AI competencies isn't confined to internal resources. Collaborations with external partners, such as academic institutions and AI-centric organizations, can bring fresh perspectives and expertise to the table. Public-private partnerships, research collaborations, and engagements with AI communities can accelerate the learning curve, keeping teams abreast of cutting-edge developments.

To measure success in developing AI competencies, organizations should establish clear metrics and benchmarks. These could include the number of AI-initiated projects, improvements in business process efficiencies, or the integration of AI-driven decisions into daily operations. Regular assessments ensure that teams' competencies evolve in line with the organization's goals and the ever-changing AI landscape.

Ultimately, the essence of nurturing AI competencies within teams lies in integrating these skills into the organizational fabric. It's about creating an environment where everyone, regardless of their role, feels empowered to contribute to the AI narrative. By developing these competencies, businesses position themselves at the forefront of innovation, fully equipped to leverage AI for substantial strategic advantage.

Fostering a Data-Driven Culture

In today's fast-paced business world, information is more than just power—it's transformative. For leaders aiming to capitalize on the potential of Artificial Intelligence, fostering a data-driven culture becomes essential. This transformation requires more than just technological adoption; it demands a paradigm shift in mindset, where decision-making processes are anchored in empirical data instead of intuition and tradition.

Leadership plays a crucial role in nurturing this shift. Leaders must not only advocate for the use of AI and data-driven methodologies but also embody them. They need to champion data literacy and empower their teams with the confidence to make informed decisions. By modeling data-centric behavior, leaders can inspire their teams to embrace and prioritize data-driven practices.

However, promoting data-driven thinking isn't merely about evangelizing its importance. It also involves equipping professionals with the tools and skills they need. Organizations must invest in training programs that enhance data literacy across all levels of the workforce. Making sense of data needs to become a part of the corporate DNA, where employees can not only interpret data but also ask the right questions around it.

An effective data-driven culture also requires robust data management systems. Ensuring that data is accurate, timely, and readily accessible allows businesses to derive insights efficiently. But accessibility is just one piece of the puzzle. Companies must also instill practices that guarantee data integrity and security, creating an environment where innovation thrives under safe conditions.

Another backbone of a data-driven culture is fostering an environment that values curiosity and critical thinking. Encouraging teams to explore, hypothesize, and question established norms can drive creativity and innovation. When employees feel their insights are valued, they are more likely to contribute meaningfully to strategically significant projects that have data at their core.

Data democratization is vital for sustaining a data-driven culture. By ensuring data isn't siloed but instead shared across departments, everyone has the chance to contribute to a holistic understanding of the business landscape. Open data policies can break down barriers, allowing for cross-functional collaboration that often leads to innovative solutions.

Moreover, organizations need to establish clear metrics for success aligned with data-driven principles. Setting measurable goals that reflect on data trends ensures that performance is tied to concrete outcomes rather than abstract targets. This approach not only drives accountability but also reinforces the value of data-driven strategies.

A key challenge in fostering a data-driven culture lies in overcoming resistance to change. Some team members might hesitate, fearing data-driven decisions could render their experience or instincts obsolete. It's crucial to approach this challenge with empathy and understanding, highlighting the synergies between human intuition and data insights while addressing fears proactively.

Incentivizing data-driven behaviors can accelerate the cultural shift. Recognizing and rewarding teams and individuals who successfully leverage data for problem-solving creates a precedent that others will strive to emulate. Such positive reinforcement fosters a competitive but collaborative atmosphere where data-centric achievements are celebrated.

Adopting a data-driven culture isn't without its pitfalls. It's essential to avoid dependency on data at the expense of creativity. While data can guide decisions, the human element is irreplaceable in interpreting results and making strategic choices. Leaders must balance data reliance with intuition for holistic decision-making.

Finally, cultivating a data-driven culture is an ongoing journey. As technologies evolve and data landscapes shift, businesses must remain agile and adaptable. Continuous learning and adaptation to new tools and practices ensure that organizations stay ahead of the curve and harness AI's full potential.

In conclusion, fostering a data-driven culture is a strategic imperative for leadership in the AI era. It requires a blend of strong leadership, comprehensive training, robust data management, and a supportive environment where data is democratized and celebrated. By weaving data into the fabric of daily operations, businesses can unlock unprecedented levels of innovation and strategic advantage, poised for success in the AI-driven future.

Chapter 14:
AI and Innovation

AI isn't just a tool for optimization; it's a catalyst for innovation, fundamentally altering how businesses conceive ideas and implement solutions. By unleashing AI's potential, organizations can explore uncharted territories, identifying opportunities that were previously invisible or deemed impossible. This transformative power of AI lies in its ability to automate cognitive tasks, enhance creative processes, and generate unprecedented insights from vast datasets. Whether it's revolutionizing product development, reimagining customer engagement, or streamlining operations, AI acts as a relentless engine, driving innovation with speed and precision. As we've seen in industries ranging from healthcare to finance, leveraging AI not only fosters a culture of innovation but also equips businesses with a strategic edge, enabling them to thrive in a competitive landscape filled with rapid technological advancements. By embracing AI, businesses don't just keep pace with change; they lead it, shaping the future of their industries and challenging the status quo.

Driving Innovation Through AI

In today's rapidly evolving business landscape, innovation isn't just a desirable asset—it's a critical necessity. For organizations striving to maintain a competitive edge, the integration of Artificial Intelligence (AI) has proven to be a substantial catalyst for innovation. AI's transformative power lies in its ability to process vast amounts of data, recognize patterns, and derive insights that would be beyond human capability. Leveraging these capabilities enables businesses to create novel products, improve services, and refine operational processes, thereby driving forward the frontier of what's possible.

AI's influence on innovation starts with its proficiency in augmenting human creativity and problem-solving abilities. This symbiosis between AI and humans allows for a new level of ideation and development. AI can rapidly scan through massive datasets, identify unmet needs, and provide insights that inspire breakthrough ideas. For instance, in product design, AI tools can simulate thousands of iterations, test variables, and recommend optimal designs based on user preferences and behavior data. By doing so, businesses not only enhance their creative processes but also significantly reduce time-to-market and associated costs.

Beyond product and service innovation, AI redefines how organizations approach customer engagement and satisfaction. It enables a deeper understanding of consumer behavior by analyzing patterns in real-time. By adopting AI-driven solutions, companies can predict trends, personalize customer experiences, and anticipate needs. This predictive capability translates to a proactive approach in fulfilling customer expectations, which can revolutionize industries ranging from retail to hospitality.

Moreover, AI's ability to foster innovation is evident in the reinvention of traditional business models. Companies are now able to exploit intelligent systems to enhance operational efficiencies, such as automating routine tasks and optimizing supply chains. This not only reduces overhead costs but also reallocates human talent to more strategic and innovative endeavors. The ability to innovate within operations ensures that businesses remain nimble and capable of responding swiftly to market changes.

A significant example of AI-driven innovation is in drug discovery and biotechnology. By employing AI algorithms, pharmaceutical companies can accelerate the development of new medications by simulating chemical reactions and interactions en masse. This reduces the time and expenses associated with lab work and testing, enabling faster transitions from theoretical models to clinical trials. Consequently, life-saving treatments reach the market more quickly, showcasing AI's potential to spearhead advancements that benefit humanity.

In the realm of sustainability and environmental innovation, AI also plays a pivotal role. Businesses are increasingly looking toward AI to enhance their sustainability initiatives. Advanced machine learning models can predict environmental impacts, optimize energy consumption, and manage waste better than traditional methods. By driving greener operations, AI not only helps companies reduce their carbon footprints but also aligns them with societal shifts towards sustainability, an increasingly crucial factor for modern consumers.

Despite its transformative potential, leveraging AI for innovation requires a careful and strategic approach. Businesses must ensure they have the right AI talent and infrastructure in place. They should focus on fostering a culture that encourages experimentation and values data-driven decision-making. An open mindset towards AI adoption is essential, as is a willingness to iterate and adapt strategies as learning occurs.

Successful innovation through AI also demands addressing the ethical and governance aspects of AI deployment. Integrating ethical considerations into the innovation process ensures that advancements do not come at the expense of privacy, security, or fairness. Companies must be transparent in how they use AI and establish frameworks to monitor and mitigate biases within AI systems to maintain trust and credibility.

As AI continues to evolve, it opens up unprecedented avenues for innovation. We can anticipate even more sophisticated AI models that might extend into designing entire businesses or developing superior problem-solving methodologies. The potential to shape the future through AI is immense, and those businesses that embrace AI-driven innovation will find themselves at the forefront of their respective industries.

In sum, driving innovation through AI is not an optional path; it is an imperative for businesses seeking sustained growth and relevance. By integrating AI into their frameworks, companies can unlock new levels of creativity, efficiency, and adaptability, paving the way for a prosperous and innovative future. By nurturing an environment that values data and AI, business leaders can ensure their organizations are equipped to tackle both existing challenges and those yet to come.

Case Studies in AI-Led Innovation

Few areas in business today hold as much promise as AI-led innovation. Companies around the globe are tapping into the potential of artificial intelligence, not just to enhance their existing processes, but to create something entirely new—pioneering products, services, and even markets that redefine what's possible. Let's dive into a series of case studies that highlight how AI is acting as a catalyst for innovation, changing the game in industries as diverse as healthcare, manufacturing, and consumer electronics.

The healthcare sector, for example, has always been ripe for innovation through AI. One company making revolutionary strides is PathAI, a firm dedicated to improving diagnostic accuracy and effectiveness through machine learning. PathAI's platform promises to detect cancer more efficiently than traditional methods by analyzing medical images with high precision. By training their algorithms on vast datasets, they've enabled pathologists to focus on complex cases, improving both the speed and accuracy of diagnoses. This AI-driven approach not only saves time but, more importantly, has the potential to save lives.

In the world of manufacturing, Siemens has harnessed AI to push the boundaries of what automated systems can achieve. By integrating AI algorithms with IoT devices on their production lines, Siemens has developed self-optimizing machines. These machines can adjust parameters such as speed and temperature in real-time based on AI predictions, leading to significant reductions in waste and energy consumption. As a result, Siemens has not only been able to enhance the quality of their products but also substantially lower costs. This kind of innovation demonstrates how AI can transform traditional industries through sustainable practices.

Consumer electronics stand as one of the most visible frontiers of AI innovation. Consider Apple's Siri, one of the first mainstream digital assistants to make a splash. Though initially met with curiosity, Siri has evolved into a core feature of Apple's ecosystem, thanks largely to continuous improvements in natural language processing powered by AI. With every iteration, Siri becomes more adept at understanding and responding to complex user requests, illustrating a seamless integration of AI into our daily lives. This AI capability core has then been leveraged across Apple's suite of products, enhancing user experience and securing its lead in the tech market.

Looking towards retail, AI's fingerprint is indelible. Take Stitch Fix, for instance. This online personal styling service combines human stylists with AI algorithms to deliver personalized clothing recommendations to customers. By using AI to analyze data from customer feedback and preferences, Stitch Fix continually optimizes its inventory and styling services. This not only caters to individual tastes but also reduces overhead costs associated with overstocking, striking a perfect balance between personalization and operational efficiency.

The automotive industry, historically seen as resistant to change, is also embracing AI as a lever for innovation. Tesla, an industry leader in this domain, employs AI to power its self-driving capabilities. Every Tesla on the road contributes data that refines and improves their autonomous systems. Such AI-driven innovation enables real-time learning and adaptation, a far cry from traditional automotive engineering methods. The result is a continuous improvement loop that not only enhances the driving experience but also edges society closer to a safer, more efficient future of personal transportation.

In the financial sector, fintech companies are redefining traditional boundaries through AI-led innovation. A notable example is Square, which employs machine learning to fend off fraudulent transactions effectively. By analyzing transaction patterns and customer behavior data in real-time, Square's AI systems can spot anomalies and potential threats faster than any human could. This proactive approach not only protects consumer and business financial interests but also builds trust, emphasizing security in a rapidly digitalizing world.

AI-led innovation is not confined to the private sector. Governments, too, are exploring AI to energize public services. For example, Singapore's Smart Nation initiative uses AI to enhance urban planning and public safety. With the help of predictive algorithms, the city-state optimizes traffic management and emergency response times. Such innovations not only improve the quality of life for its citizens but also set a benchmark for other nations contemplating similar strides towards smarter cities.

The entrepreneurial spirit finds a new ally in AI as startups leverage this technology for disruptive innovation. Consider OpenAI's trailblazing work with natural language models, which has influenced industries ranging from entertainment to education. The ripple effect of their pioneering models is enormous, leading to new applications and user experiences that were inconceivable just a few years ago.

Through strategic partnerships with enterprises, OpenAI is fostering an environment where creativity and technology intersect, driving forward a new era of digital transformation.

These case studies underscore a critical insight: AI is not just a tool for enhancing efficiency. It's an enabler of new business models, offering fresh pathways to value creation. By fostering environments where AI can thrive, businesses can achieve breakthroughs that were once beyond the realm of possibility. Yet, this requires a deliberate strategy that aligns AI capabilities with a company's vision and market dynamics—a subject we will elaborate on in other sections of this book.

As we consider the transformative potential of AI, it becomes clear that the frontier of innovation is boundless. For business leaders, the key lies in tweaking their mindset to embrace AI not as a replacement for human ingenuity, but as a collaborative partner in the quest for innovation. The companies leading the charge today exemplify how AI can seamlessly integrate into their strategies to spearhead truly revolutionary changes.

In conclusion, AI-led innovation represents an extraordinary opportunity for businesses willing to invest in the technology, culture, and processes required to harness its potential fully. While challenges in implementation and ethical considerations persist, the examples highlighted in these case studies illustrate that AI can be a powerful ally in the ongoing journey towards an innovative, sustainable, and competitive future. Innovation driven by AI will undoubtedly be one of the compelling narratives of our time, shaping a landscape where companies that master this capability will thrive.

Chapter 15:
Competitive Advantage with AI

In today's rapidly evolving business landscape, harnessing AI for competitive advantage is more crucial than ever. Organizations that deftly integrate AI into their core strategies can unlock unprecedented capabilities, setting themselves apart in crowded markets. By leveraging AI, businesses can not only strengthen their market position through innovative products and services but also refine their operational efficiencies, ensuring they stay ahead of industry trends. The key lies in differentiating through AI technology, which allows for custom-tailored solutions that resonate with customer needs and expectations. This technological edge fosters a cycle of continuous improvement, enhancing decision-making processes and driving sustainable growth. As AI becomes an integral part of strategic frameworks, it transforms how businesses approach problem-solving, revealing opportunities that weren't visible before. The journey toward AI-driven market dominance is not merely about adopting the latest technology but about fostering a culture of innovation and agility that will position enterprises to thrive amidst change.

Leveraging AI for Market Dominance

The business landscape is witnessing a seismic shift, driven by the relentless advancement of Artificial Intelligence technologies. Companies that seek to gain a foothold—or maintain their current stronghold—must prioritize leveraging AI as a cornerstone for market dominance. AI has transformed from a niche tool for tech-savvy companies to an essential asset for businesses striving to outmaneuver competitors. Its capabilities extend beyond mere process enhancements to unlocking new revenue streams and reshaping customer experiences, thereby offering unparalleled opportunities for securing a competitive advantage.

Business leaders are increasingly recognizing that AI offers a dual advantage: market resilience and expansion. This dual advantage comes from AI's intrinsic capability to innovate and optimize simultaneously. It can help businesses automate mundane processes and explore uncharted territories, from intuitive customer interfaces to anticipating market demands with surprising accuracy. Companies that effectively harness AI find themselves not only resilient in the face of market disruptions but also capable of capitalizing on these changes as growth opportunities.

The journey toward AI-enabled market dominance begins with a robust strategy—one rooted in a deep understanding of AI capabilities and their alignment with business goals. By clearly defining objectives and deploying AI in strategic areas, companies can differentiate themselves in increasingly crowded markets. A strategic approach involves identifying core business areas where AI can offer the most value, whether through enhancing product features, personalizing customer interactions, or optimizing supply chain logistics.

An integral part of leveraging AI is understanding customer behavior at an unprecedented level. Through advanced analytics and machine learning, businesses can sift through massive data troves to uncover patterns and trends that were previously hidden. These insights empower companies to tailor their products and services to meet evolving consumer needs, thereby fostering customer loyalty and enhancing brand reputation. Personalized experiences, driven by AI, not only improve customer satisfaction but also create a barrier for competitors who lack similar capabilities.

Moreover, AI fosters agility, allowing businesses to respond swiftly to market changes and consumer preferences. In a world where consumer demands shift rapidly, agility is akin to flexibility—it can make or break a company's market position. Agile companies leverage AI to iterate quickly on products, services, and strategies, continuously enhancing their offerings based on real-time feedback and insights. As a result, they can outpace slower movers and capture market share more effectively.

Investment in AI is not merely about technology acquisition; it's about cultivating an innovation-driven culture. Companies can achieve this by fostering an environment that encourages experimentation and learning. Such a culture promotes the seamless integration of AI into business processes. Teams equipped with the right skills and mindset are more likely to unleash AI's potential, driving the company toward sustainable growth. A culture of innovation helps organizations stay ahead by creating products and services that anticipate customer needs before they arise.

While technology provides the tools, leadership plays a critical role in wielding these tools effectively. Forward-thinking leaders who prioritize AI initiatives can establish a significant lead over competitors. They align AI projects with strategic priorities, ensuring that their impact resonates throughout the organization. Leaders who champion AI-driven market dominance are instrumental in accelerating adoption and securing stakeholder buy-in. Their advocacy not only demystifies AI's potential within the organization but also galvanizes teams to engage with AI projects enthusiastically.

Clearly defined key performance indicators (KPIs) are essential in measuring the success of AI implementation. They help assess the effectiveness of AI initiatives in achieving business goals and provide a framework for continuous improvement. By regularly reviewing and adjusting these KPIs, businesses can ensure that their AI deployments remain aligned with changing market dynamics and organizational priorities.

Innovation and competitive advantage go hand in hand, and AI is at their confluence. Businesses that leverage AI to foster innovation position themselves as leaders rather than followers in their respective industries. AI's ability to drive product innovation, optimize operations, and transform customer experiences is unparalleled. Companies that recognize and act on this potential are not just achieving market dominance; they're defining the standards across sectors, setting benchmarks for others to follow.

In conclusion, leveraging AI for market dominance is not a one-time effort but a continuous strategic journey. It requires a vision that aligns technology with business objectives, a culture that embraces innovation, and leadership that champions AI initiatives. As AI continues to evolve, its role in shaping market landscapes will only grow. Companies that seize the opportunity to incorporate AI strategically will redefine their competitive edges and secure their places as market leaders.

Differentiating Through AI Technology

In today's hyper-competitive business environment, leveraging artificial intelligence to gain a unique competitive edge isn't just a possibility; it's a necessity. As markets evolve, AI can serve as a powerful differentiator, setting businesses apart with strategic innovation and agility. While many enterprises begin their AI journey focusing on operational efficiency or predictive analytics, true differentiation comes from embedding AI technologies at the core of business strategy where they can unlock unprecedented value.

To differentiate through AI, businesses need to think beyond incremental improvements. The most successful companies are those that dare to reimagine their business models, often using AI to create entirely new customer experiences, products, or even markets. For instance, AI can enable a retailer not only to predict inventory needs but also to personalize the shopping experience in real-time, tailoring it to individual preferences through dynamic adjustments in product offerings and pricing. Such personalization, powered by deep learning algorithms that process vast amounts of data, can turn one-time buyers into loyal customers.

It's the agility of AI that provides another layer of differentiation. Traditional business processes, no matter how finely tuned, often lack the ability to quickly adapt to changes in market conditions or consumer behavior. AI systems, however, can rapidly assimilate new data, continually learning and optimizing decision-making processes. This dynamic adaptability doesn't just support existing operations; it can redefine them. Consider the way AI-driven robots and automated systems in manufacturing adjust workflows and predict maintenance needs, significantly reducing downtime and costs.

Customization is the essence of an AI-driven competitive strategy. By harnessing AI's ability to analyze large datasets, businesses can craft micro-strategies tailored to distinct segments, geographies, or even individual customers, which can be scaled with minimal additional cost. Customer data is analyzed not only to understand past behavior but to predict future needs and preferences. When supported by AI technologies, companies can launch targeted marketing campaigns, design bespoke products, and even anticipatory services—creating a seamless, engaging client journey across multiple touchpoints.

Innovation driven by AI technology can also lead to unique product development cycles. AI shortens the time from conception to market by simulating and testing new ideas rapidly through virtual models and prototypes. This capability isn't confined to large enterprises; small and medium-sized enterprises (SMEs), by leveraging cloud-based AI solutions, can access powerful analytics and computational resources previously available only to larger organizations. This democratization of AI is, in itself, a transformative force that enables new market entrants to challenge incumbents. With AI, SMEs can innovate quickly, disrupt traditional industries, and take advantage of niches overlooked by larger competitors.

Furthermore, AI-enhanced decision-making processes enable businesses to identify emerging trends before they become mainstream. By analyzing social media, purchasing patterns, and industry reports, AI systems can offer insights into potential market shifts. This foresight allows companies to be proactive rather than reactive, positioning themselves advantageously against competitors who rely on traditional market analysis. Early adopters of AI are often the ones setting industry standards, influencing future regulatory norms, and establishing a significant early-mover advantage.

An organization's internal culture can also be a differentiator when AI technologies are involved. A culture committed to continuous learning and innovation nurtures curiosity and openness to new ideas, essential for successfully integrating AI into daily operations. Leadership plays a crucial role in shaping such a culture by fostering an environment where experimentation with AI technologies is encouraged, knowledge sharing is promoted, and failures are seen as opportunities to learn and grow. This adaptive cultural approach can be far more effective than a one-size-fits-all method and can give a substantial strategic advantage over less agile competitors.

Nevertheless, differentiation through AI also comes with challenges, notably the ethical considerations businesses must navigate. As AI systems become more sophisticated, ensuring that they do not inadvertently perpetuate biases or compromise data security becomes paramount. It is the companies that focus on these ethical considerations—embedding fairness and transparency into their AI systems—that will not only secure a competitive advantage but also gain trust and loyalty from their customers and partners. By prioritizing ethical AI, organizations build more meaningful connections with their audiences, elevating brand integrity.

In conclusion, differentiation through AI is more than just technological integration; it's a transformative strategy that encompasses reshaping the very essence of business models, customer engagement, and market dynamics. By embracing AI with a bold vision, businesses can create a unique identity in the marketplace, achieve operational excellence, and foster a culture of innovation. These enterprises don't just survive; they thrive, leveraging AI as a catalyst for long-term growth and leadership in their respective fields. The next chapter will delve further into the intricacies of leveraging AI for market dominance, exploring additional frameworks and strategies tailored for outperforming the competition in an ever-evolving digital landscape.

Chapter 16:
AI in Customer Experience

In today's hyper-competitive market, businesses are rapidly leveraging AI technologies to revolutionize customer experience, transforming it from a standard transaction into a deeply personalized journey. By harnessing data-driven insights and predictive analytics, AI enables companies to anticipate customer needs and preferences with impressive accuracy, leading to enhanced user engagement and satisfaction. This personalized interaction not only fosters customer loyalty but also drives value creation, as businesses better understand and adapt to the dynamic demands of their clientele. Moreover, AI-powered tools like chatbots and virtual assistants streamline customer support, offering timely and efficient resolutions to queries while freeing up human resources for more complex problem-solving tasks. As AI continues to evolve, its integration into customer experience strategies promises not just optimization but a profound rethinking of how businesses connect with their customers, laying the groundwork for sustained competitive advantage in an ever-changing digital landscape.

Enhancing User Engagement with AI

In an era where businesses are consistently seeking to differentiate themselves and capture the attention of consumers, Artificial Intelligence (AI) stands out as a pivotal tool for enhancing user engagement in unprecedented ways. Companies today are leveraging

AI to create personalized, dynamic, and real-time interactions with their customers, significantly enhancing the user experience. This transformation is not just about adopting new technologies but about reimagining the way businesses interact with their customers in the digital age.

At the core of this evolution is the capacity of AI to process and analyze vast amounts of data quickly and accurately. By doing so, organizations can gain deeper insights into customer preferences, behaviors, and needs. This understanding allows businesses to offer highly personalized experiences that were once thought impossible. Personalized recommendations, for example, are now a staple on e-commerce platforms, resulting in not only increased engagement but also higher conversion rates. The key lies in AI's ability to learn and adapt over time, continually refining its outputs and predictions.

AI-driven engagement isn't just limited to shopping and recommendations. In the entertainment industry, for instance, streaming services use AI algorithms to curate content based on individual viewing habits. This intelligent content curation keeps users engaged and loyal to the platform, reducing churn and enhancing customer satisfaction. AI doesn't just make assumptions based on demographics; it goes further, analyzing real-time data to predict what each user might enjoy next, thus keeping them continually interacting with the service.

Moreover, AI is revolutionizing customer service, transforming it from a reactive function into a proactive engagement strategy. AI-powered chatbots and virtual assistants are now ubiquitous, handling a significant portion of customer inquiries without human intervention. These tools not only provide instant responses, improving customer satisfaction but also free up human agents to focus on more complex issues. Virtual assistants can also engage with customers across various platforms, be it through social media, messaging apps, or websites, providing a seamless service experience that enhances engagement.

Incorporating sentiment analysis into AI systems is another game-changer. Businesses can tap into AI to monitor social media streams and customer feedback in real-time, identifying shifts in sentiment and potential issues before they escalate. This capability empowers brands to engage with users in a timely and relevant manner, addressing concerns proactively and maintaining a positive brand image. It's about creating a dialogue with customers, rather than a monologue, fostering a sense of community and loyalty around the brand.

Furthermore, augmented reality (AR) and AI are converging to create immersive and interactive experiences. Retail companies are utilizing AI to power AR try-ons, allowing users to visualize products like furniture or clothing in their own space before making a purchase. This interactive engagement not only captures user interest but also helps convert interest into sales. The technology acts as an engaging tool that can set a brand apart by offering something unique and memorable.

Implementing AI to enhance user engagement also contributes to the overall customer journey, ensuring that every touchpoint is optimized and cohesive. From initial contact to post-purchase support, AI can guide users through a seamless and personalized journey. Dynamic content delivery, tailored email campaigns, and predictive customer journey mapping reshape how businesses maintain engagement and foster long-term relationships with their clients.

Yet, the road to fully embracing AI in user engagement is not without hurdles. Privacy concerns loom large in the minds of consumers, requiring businesses to navigate carefully between personalization and privacy. Ethical considerations regarding data usage must be taken seriously, with transparency and user consent at the forefront of any AI engagement strategy. Trust is paramount, and companies need to ensure that AI-driven engagements maintain the highest standards of ethical responsibility.

As we look forward, the potential for AI to enhance user engagement will only grow. Emerging technologies like AI in virtual reality (VR) and advanced machine learning models promise to open new dimensions of interaction. Businesses that can effectively harness these technologies will not only engage users more deeply but will also position themselves ahead of the competition.

In conclusion, AI is not just a tool for automating processes or generating insights; it is a powerful catalyst for transforming how businesses engage with their customers. By enhancing personalization, streamlining interactions, and predicting user needs, AI offers a pathway to richer, more meaningful customer relationships. As businesses continue to innovate and adopt these technologies, the future of customer engagement looks brighter than ever, marked by creativity, connectivity, and enhanced customer loyalty. Ultimately, those who master the integration of AI into their engagement strategies will thrive in today's competitive landscape.

AI for Customer Support Optimization

Customer support is a crucial touchpoint between businesses and their customers. It's where empathy meets efficiency, and expectations are high. As enterprises recognize the transformative potential of AI, the focus on optimizing customer support using AI technologies has become more pronounced. The goal is not only to meet customer inquiries but to exceed them, creating loyal advocates from satisfied customers. This shift toward AI integration in customer support encompasses multiple facets and offers an array of benefits, from significantly reducing response times to enhancing the quality of interactions.

One of the key elements in AI-driven customer support optimization is automation. AI tools like chatbots and virtual agents have revolutionized the initial interaction phase by efficiently handling a myriad of customer queries without human intervention. These AI systems can address common questions, troubleshoot simple issues, and route complex inquiries to the appropriate human agents. The effect is a streamlined experience where basic inquiries are resolved promptly, freeing human agents to focus on more complex cases that require nuanced understanding and empathy.

For AI to truly optimize customer support, understanding and accuracy are paramount. Natural Language Processing (NLP) plays a pivotal role here. This branch of AI enables systems to comprehend, interpret, and respond to human language in a way that's both meaningful and contextually relevant. The ability of AI to 'understand' customer communications means that responses are not only faster but also more precise. NLP technology continuously evolves through learning, permitting the systems to improve over time and adapt to changing customer language patterns and behavior.

Moreover, sentiment analysis further bolsters AI's ability to enhance customer support. By analyzing the tone and emotion in customer messages, AI can gauge satisfaction levels, predicting when a customer might feel frustrated or happy. This insight allows customer service teams to prioritize responses based on the urgency inferred from sentiment levels, providing a more timely and empathetic support system. It also helps businesses gather insights into customer sentiments at a macro level, informing potential changes in products or services.

Data also plays a pivotal role in refining AI-driven customer support strategies. By examining historical data, AI can predict future issues and have preemptively prepared responses or solutions. This capability not only speeds up response times but also positions

113

businesses to avert potential issues before they escalate. With machine learning algorithms analyzing customer data, AI can identify patterns and anomalies, allowing support teams to proactively address concerns and enhance the customer journey.

Personalization is another avenue through which AI optimizes customer support. Utilizing machine learning algorithms, AI can tailor interactions based on customer's past behavior, preferences, and history with the brand. This personalized approach not only makes the customer feel valued but can also lead to increased satisfaction and loyalty. By utilizing AI to analyze customer data, businesses can craft unique experiences that resonate with individual customers, encouraging repeat business and long-lasting relationships.

Implementing AI in customer support doesn't only benefit the customer; it creates efficiency within the organization. The automation of routine tasks, such as ticket categorization and initial diagnostics, allows support staff to focus on higher-value activities. This reallocation of resources can lead to increased job satisfaction for customer support staff, as they engage in more challenging problem-solving tasks that leverage their skills and expertise fully. This evolution in job roles also fosters a stronger bond between staff and technology, encouraging a collaborative environment that blends human intuition with AI precision.

While the advantages of AI in customer support are evident, there are challenges that businesses must navigate to optimize its implementation. Chief among these is ensuring data privacy and security. When handling customer data, AI systems must adhere to stringent data protection standards, safeguarding against breaches and misuse. This obligation requires constant vigilance and investment in security protocols to build trust with customers. Moreover, addressing operation biases in AI algorithms is imperative to ensure fair treatment and support across diverse customer demographics.

AI-driven customer support also necessitates a continuous improvement mindset. Technologies and customers evolve, and businesses must remain agile in updating their AI systems. Feedback loops play a critical role in this process, where constant monitoring and refinement ensure that the AI tools remain relevant and effective. Regular audits and updates help businesses keep their systems aligned with best practices and evolving customer expectations.

The journey of AI optimization in customer support is not just about deploying tools but rather weaving them into the strategic fabric of the organization. Success requires a vision that aligns technology with human skills to create a seamless, responsive, and empathetic support system. Businesses need to train staff not only to use AI technologies but to work alongside them, creating an ecosystem where AI's capabilities enhance human strengths.

Ultimately, AI for customer support optimization is more than a technological advancement; it's a strategic opportunity for businesses to redefine their relationship with customers. By harnessing AI's power, companies can deliver exceptional service efficiently and innovatively, cultivating a customer experience that's not only consistent but also inspired. In today's competitive landscape, where customer loyalty is a critical marker of success, AI offers a clear path to creating experiences that leave lasting impressions, turning service into a strategic advantage.

Chapter 17:
Regulatory and Legal Aspects

As businesses increasingly integrate artificial intelligence into their operations, understanding the evolving regulatory and legal landscape becomes essential for strategic decision-making. With AI rapidly transforming industries, navigating the myriad of regulations ensures compliance and mitigates risks. Business leaders must stay informed of new legislation impacting AI technologies, such as data protection laws and industry-specific guidelines, which can vary widely across regions. Understanding these legal frameworks helps companies harness AI's potential while avoiding costly legal pitfalls. It's vital for organizations to establish robust governance frameworks that address data privacy and security, fostering a culture of transparency and ethical AI usage. By proactively engaging with regulators and participating in shaping policies, businesses not only safeguard their operations but also position themselves as industry leaders. This strategic foresight ensures that AI implementations are not only legally sound but also aligned with global best practices, propelling organizations toward sustainable growth and competitive advantage.

Navigating AI Regulations

The landscape of artificial intelligence is evolving at an unprecedented pace, and businesses are racing to leverage its potential. Yet, as we embrace innovation, understanding the regulatory environment that governs AI is crucial. Inadequate compliance can lead to legal challenges, financial penalties, and reputational damage, making it imperative for business leaders to navigate AI regulations effectively. This section will explore strategies and considerations essential for aligning AI initiatives with the regulatory frameworks in various markets.

Governments and regulatory bodies across the globe are grappling with how to manage the rapid advancements in AI. The European Union's proposed AI Act, for instance, aims to classify AI applications by risk level, imposing stricter obligations on high-risk applications. Similar regulatory movements are unfolding in other jurisdictions, each with unique approaches to balancing innovation with risk mitigation. For businesses, understanding these nuances and anticipating regulatory changes is not just a compliance issue—it's a strategic necessity.

First and foremost, companies need to integrate compliance into their AI strategy from the ground up. This involves establishing a dedicated team or appointing a compliance officer responsible for keeping abreast of regulatory developments. Regular audits and assessments should be conducted to ensure that AI systems meet the latest standards and guidelines. Moreover, embedding ethical considerations into AI processes can not only help in adhering to regulations but also in building trust with stakeholders.

One of the key regulatory challenges businesses face is data protection. Machine learning algorithms thrive on vast amounts of data, which often include personal and sensitive information. With regulations like the General Data Protection Regulation (GDPR) setting stringent requirements for data handling, businesses must implement robust data governance frameworks. This involves ensuring that data collection, storage, and processing activities are transparent and consented to by individuals. It also requires maintaining data accuracy and facilitating data subject rights, such as access and erasure.

Another critical area of focus is algorithmic accountability. As AI systems gain autonomy, their decision-making processes become more opaque and complex. Regulators are increasingly demanding transparency and explainability, especially in sectors like finance, healthcare, and autonomous vehicles. To comply, companies should invest in methods that improve the interpretability of AI outcomes. Tools that provide insight into the decision-making process not only aid compliance but also enhance business decision-making by providing clarity and justification for AI-driven actions.

Additionally, bias and discrimination in AI are significant concerns that regulators are beginning to address. AI systems trained on biased data can perpetuate and even amplify inequality, leading to unfair outcomes. To mitigate these risks, businesses should employ fair data practices and continually monitor AI systems for bias. Conducting regular fairness assessments and involving diverse teams in AI development can help identify potential biases, ensuring that AI solutions are equitable and inclusive.

The legal implications of AI malfunction or harm also demand careful attention. Determining liability can be a complex endeavor when autonomous systems operate beyond human supervision. Businesses need to establish clear protocols for accountability and should consider engaging legal experts to navigate these novel challenges. Insurance coverage tailored for AI-related risks can provide an additional layer of protection, safeguarding the enterprise from unforeseen legal disputes.

Globally, the harmonization of AI regulations remains a challenge. For multinational corporations, differing regulatory landscapes can lead to a convoluted compliance strategy. A proactive approach involves fostering strong relationships with regulators and participating in international forums to influence and stay informed on regulatory trends. By engaging in dialogue with policymakers, businesses can help shape regulations that are both conducive to innovation and protective of societal interests.

Moreover, staying ahead of regulatory requirements requires continuous education and adaptation. Training programs for employees at all levels can enhance understanding and adherence to AI laws, ensuring that compliance permeates the organizational culture. Leveraging insights from legal experts and compliance technology can streamline efforts, providing scalable solutions for regulatory adherence.

Finally, businesses must be agile in their regulatory strategies. As the regulatory landscape for AI evolves, so too must the policies and practices of companies deploying AI solutions. Developing a flexible regulatory framework that can adapt to new guidelines will be key to maintaining competitive advantage while adhering to the rule of law. This includes regularly updating internal policies, maintaining open lines of communication with regulatory bodies, and being prepared to pivot as needed in response to legislative changes.

In conclusion, navigating AI regulations requires not only an understanding of current laws but also a foresight for future developments. By embedding compliance into the core of AI strategies, businesses can unlock the full potential of AI while safeguarding against risks. A proactive and informed approach will empower organizations to turn regulatory challenges into opportunities for growth, innovation, and sustained competitive advantage.

Understanding Legal Implications

The rise of artificial intelligence (AI) in the business world introduces a complex network of legal implications that leaders can no longer afford to overlook. As AI technologies become deeply embedded in enterprise decision-making processes, understanding these implications is vital for leveraging their benefits while minimizing potential liabilities. Companies are now faced with the task of navigating an evolving legal landscape where regulations struggle to keep up with technological advancements.

One of the most pressing concerns in the realm of AI legality is compliance with data protection laws. The General Data Protection Regulation (GDPR) in the European Union and the California Consumer Privacy Act (CCPA) in the United States are prime examples of how stringent data privacy laws are actively shaping AI practices. These regulations stipulate that businesses must uphold consumers' rights to data privacy and ensure lawful processing, collection, and storage of personal information. Non-compliance could result in hefty fines and reputational damage, making it imperative for enterprises to incorporate these legal standards into their AI strategies from the ground up.

Moreover, AI systems frequently rely on vast datasets that may inadvertently include biases. Businesses are increasingly held accountable for the ethical and legal responsibility of the AI-generated decisions. While AI can streamline processes and enhance decision accuracy, it can also perpetuate existing biases or introduce new ones, leading to discriminatory outcomes. Lawsuits over biased AI decisions are becoming more common, where enterprises can face significant legal challenges, especially in sectors like recruitment, loan approvals, and policing.

Intellectual property (IP) rights present another intricate aspect of AI legality. As AI systems contribute to creating content, generating inventions, or composing music, delineating ownership of the AI-created properties becomes complex. Current IP laws aren't adequately equipped to address the nuances of machine-generated innovations. This presents both legal challenges and opportunities as businesses navigate ownership claims, seek patent protections, or license AI-generated content.

The liability of autonomous systems further complicates the legal landscape for businesses integrating AI. In scenarios where AI systems operate independently, such as autonomous vehicles or automated trading platforms, determining liability in the event of a malfunction or accident is challenging. Organizations need to prepare for potential legal disputes surrounding AI system-induced damage, as well as explore insurance solutions that cover AI-related risks.

Another key consideration is antitrust laws. As AI can provide substantial competitive advantages, regulators are actively examining how these technologies impact market competition. There are ongoing discussions and legal considerations around AI's role in creating monopolistic scenarios or unfair market practices. For business leaders, adhering to antitrust laws while pursuing AI-driven market dominance is a balancing act that requires careful strategic planning.

Labor laws are also brought into question with escalating AI adoption. Automation and AI have led to significant changes in the workforce, challenging existing employment laws. Organizations must consider the legal implications of workforce restructuring due to AI technologies, which can impact employment contracts, job security, and worker rights. Engaging with labor unions and conducting transparent dialogues with employees will be critical to ensuring ethical and legal compliance in this context.

With AI being used in various sensitive applications, from healthcare to finance, regulatory bodies worldwide are formulating comprehensive AI guidelines aimed at protecting consumers and maintaining societal trust. These guidelines often serve as a framework for businesses to align their AI practices with legal expectations. Remaining informed and adaptive to such regulatory developments is essential for enterprises seeking to maintain compliance and avoid legal entanglements.

Seeking legal counsel specializing in AI and technology is becoming increasingly important for businesses embarking on AI-led transformations. Legal experts can provide guidance on everything from compliance with international data laws to navigating potential liability issues. Establishing a robust legal framework is not just about risk mitigation but also about viewing compliance as a strategic advantage that can differentiate a business in crowded markets.

Ultimately, understanding and addressing the legal implications of AI isn't a one-off exercise but an ongoing process that requires vigilance and adaptability. As AI continues to evolve, so too will its legal intricacies. Business leaders must ensure they have flexible strategies and policies in place, allowing them to quickly adapt to emerging legal and ethical standards. Embracing a proactive approach to legal developments in AI can not only protect an organization from potential liabilities but also position it for sustainable, responsible growth.

Chapter 18:
Future Trends in AI

As we venture into the future of Artificial Intelligence, business leaders find themselves on the threshold of transformation brought about by astonishing technological advancements. AI is not just evolving; it's revolutionizing how decisions are made, reshaping industry standards, and unlocking unprecedented opportunities for growth. We're witnessing the emergence of cutting-edge technologies like quantum computing, which promises to exponentially increase processing power, and the progress of embodied AI in robotics, giving rise to more intuitive and immersive human-machine interactions. The predictive capabilities of AI are also reaching new heights, empowering enterprises to forecast market shifts with remarkable precision. Strategically harnessing these emergent trends will position businesses not only to adapt but to thrive by creating innovative pathways to competitive advantage. The key lies in staying informed and agile, ready to embrace the dynamic changes AI will undoubtedly continue to unleash across global sectors.

Emerging Technologies in AI

As we look forward to the future landscape of Artificial Intelligence, the horizon gleams with disruptive technologies that promise to reshape industries and redefine possibilities. Emerging technologies in AI are not just enhancements—some of them radically alter how we perceive and interact with the digital world. These advancements, still in the nascent stages, offer tantalizing prospects for businesses aiming to leverage AI for a competitive edge. Understanding them can empower companies to stay ahead in an ever-evolving marketplace.

One of the most compelling advancements is the development of neuromorphic computing. Mimicking the neural structure of the human brain, this technology is designed to process data more efficiently, reducing power consumption and increasing processing speeds dramatically. For businesses, this means AI systems could soon operate more sustainably, delivering faster insights with a fraction of the energy cost. Neuromorphic computing paves the way for more potent machine learning models, enhancing real-time data analysis and decision-making capabilities.

Quantum computing represents another front where AI advancements are taking giant strides. While still largely experimental, quantum computers promise unparalleled processing capabilities by utilizing principles of quantum mechanics. They have the potential to solve complex problems beyond the reach of classical computers. For business leaders, this might eventually allow for groundbreaking developments in optimization, cryptography, and complex system simulations. Companies investing in quantum research today are hopeful for revolutionary benefits once the technology becomes more mature and accessible.

Edge AI, where data processing and analysis happen at the point of data generation, rather than in centralized data centers, is gaining tremendous traction. As businesses generate vast amounts of data from IoT devices, the need for real-time responses is critical. Edge AI reduces latency, enhances security by minimizing data transfer risks, and ensures better utilization of bandwidth. This evolution facilitates smarter cities, refined industrial automation, and more responsive consumer products. For decision-makers, Edge AI promises to enhance operational efficiency and customer satisfaction dramatically.

The intersection of AI and biotechnology is another exciting domain, especially with the rise of personalized medicine. Thanks to AI's capabilities to analyze massive genomics datasets, biotech firms are now developing bespoke treatment plans tailored to individuals' genetic makeup. Such advancements hold the promise of not just treating, but predicting and preventing diseases more effectively. In the broader business context, sectors like pharmaceuticals and healthcare are witnessing a paradigm shift in how treatments are developed and delivered, heralding a new era of precision healthcare.

Natural Language Processing (NLP) continues to evolve, with emerging algorithms pushing the boundaries of human-computer interaction. New models are getting better at understanding and generating human language, offering real-time translation services, and creating avenues for more intuitive and seamless communication with AI systems. Businesses leverage these advancements for enhanced customer support, improved content generation, and more insightful data analysis. As AI becomes more adept at understanding human language nuances, the potential for personalized customer experiences grows exponentially.

Another promising sector is the proliferation of autonomous systems. From self-driving cars to automated drones, these technologies are increasingly integrated into various industries. For businesses, such advancements in robotics and automation can lead to optimized supply chain management, reduced operational costs, and increased safety standards. Autonomous systems are reshaping logistics, agriculture, and even sectors like security and monitoring, creating new paradigms of efficiency and reliability.

Generative AI, or AI systems that can create, is pushing the envelope of creativity and innovation in fields such as design, entertainment, and content creation. These systems can autonomously produce images, music, and even complex reports. Businesses are tapping into these capabilities to accelerate product development cycles, experiment with new content ideas, and customize offerings for diverse consumer bases. The implications of Generative AI are profound, heralding an era where machines are not just tools for computation but collaborators in creativity.

The continual integration of AI with cloud technologies also stands out as a transformative force. Cloud AI democratizes access to advanced machine learning models and computational resources, allowing small businesses to compete with larger enterprises in data-driven innovations. As AI services become more accessible on cloud platforms, companies of all sizes can leverage powerful analytics, streamline operations, and enhance customer experiences without significant infrastructure investments.

Lastly, sustainability is becoming a core focus of AI advancements. AI technologies are now being developed and deployed with an emphasis on environmental impact, aiding businesses in their quest for sustainability goals. From optimizing energy consumption in data centers to enabling precision agriculture that reduces resource waste, AI is integral to sustainable innovation. As regulatory pressures and consumer awareness heighten, sustainable AI not only drives operational efficiency but also enhances corporate responsibility and brand reputation.

In conclusion, emerging technologies in AI offer a dynamic and challenging yet rewarding landscape for business leaders. Embracing these innovations will require a willingness to explore, experiment, and adapt, but the potential rewards are unprecedented. Businesses that strategically integrate these technologies stand to redefine their industries and craft a future where AI-driven insights and efficiencies are at the core of their competitive advantage.

Predicting the Next Big Changes

As we stand on the brink of a new AI era, the potential for transformative change is immense. We are entering a phase where artificial intelligence is poised to redefine industries and create paradigms that were previously unimaginable. To effectively leverage AI for a strategic edge, business leaders must not only comprehend current capabilities but also anticipate the shifts that will inevitably come.

One of the most promising areas is the integration of AI with emerging technologies like quantum computing. Quantum computing has the potential to exponentially speed up data processing and problem-solving capabilities. This fusion could revolutionize industries by handling complex calculations that are currently beyond classical systems. For instance, it might solve intricate logistical problems and make breakthroughs in fields such as materials science and pharmaceuticals. Being able to foresee how these technologies will converge offers businesses a significant competitive advantage.

Another trend is the evolution of AI from narrow capabilities to more general, human-like intelligence. While current AI systems excel at specific tasks, the next leap could be towards systems that mimic the breadth and adaptability of human cognition. This means AI could tackle a wider array of problems and offer solutions across varied contexts without extensive retraining. Businesses should be prepared to harness this versatility, creating systems that are agile and can adapt to a range of challenges in real-time.

AI's role in cybersecurity cannot be overstated. As cyber threats become more sophisticated, AI will increasingly be deployed to predict, identify, and neutralize attacks before they can cause damage. The future will likely see AI-driven security systems that can learn from each attempted breach to fortify defenses against future threats. Businesses that proactively incorporate AI into their security strategies will not only protect themselves against potential losses but also build a trust-worthy digital environment for their customers.

In parallel, the personalization of AI interactions is set to deepen. The next wave of AI will not just react to data input but will foresee customer needs and adapt interactions accordingly. This predictiveness can vastly enhance customer experiences, particularly in marketing and customer support. Imagine AI systems that anticipate customer concerns before they articulate them, offering solutions or product suggestions that align perfectly with individual preferences and past behaviors. This level of personalization will redefine customer expectations and set a new standard for service excellence.

Automation, powered by AI, will further reshape the workforce of the future, but with added layers of sophistication and responsibility. Initial fears about job displacement are giving way to more nuanced discussions about the nature of work. The focus is shifting toward a harmonious collaboration between humans and machines, where AI assumes repetitive tasks and humans are free to engage in more creative and strategic pursuits. Organizations will need to tailor their training and development programs to foster new skills and roles, emphasizing creativity, emotional intelligence, and strategic thinking.

The role of AI in fostering sustainability is another crucial frontier. AI algorithms can optimize energy use across production and distribution channels, aid in predicting and mitigating the effects of climate change, and drive efficiency in resource management. Businesses that can integrate AI into their sustainability initiatives not only contribute to a healthier planet but also position themselves as innovators in an increasingly eco-conscious marketplace.

Furthermore, the potential for AI to impact healthcare continues to grow. We anticipate advancements in AI-driven diagnostics, personalized medicine, and robotic surgery, among others. AI could enable unprecedented levels of disease prediction and prevention, potentially transforming global health outcomes. For healthcare enterprises, the imperative will be to integrate these advances into their practices, ensuring that they can offer cutting-edge services while navigating complex regulatory landscapes.

With these exciting developments come new ethical, regulatory, and privacy considerations. As AI systems become more autonomous and impactful, ensuring that they operate within ethical guidelines and respect user privacy is critical. Businesses will need to establish robust governance structures to manage the ethical implications of their AI operations, balancing innovation with accountability.

Ultimately, predicting the next big changes in AI requires a forward-thinking mindset. Organizations that remain agile and are willing to invest in ongoing learning and adaptation will be better positioned to capitalize on these changes. By fostering a culture of openness to innovation and collaboration with diverse technological advances, businesses can ensure they are not just adapting to the future, but actively shaping it. In this dynamic era of AI, the ability to anticipate and adapt will be the linchpin of sustained success and leadership.

Chapter 19:
Measuring AI Impact

Measuring the impact of AI initiatives is crucial for any business that aspires to stay competitive and innovative in today's fast-paced environment. At the core of assessing AI's success are key performance indicators (KPIs), carefully designed to track progress and quantify benefits such as cost reduction, revenue growth, and enhanced customer satisfaction. While these metrics provide a snapshot of AI's contribution to your business goals, a deeper analysis of return on investment (ROI) reveals the nuanced value AI brings across various dimensions of operations and strategy. Successful measurement involves integrating both quantitative and qualitative assessments, encouraging a holistic view that underscores AI's transformative potential. By leveraging data analytics along with strategic insights, companies can fine-tune their AI strategies, thus paving the way for sustained competitive advantage. Embracing this measurement mindset transforms AI from a buzzword into a tangible driver of growth, innovation, and value creation.

KPIs for AI Success

In a rapidly evolving digital landscape, understanding how to measure the success of artificial intelligence initiatives is crucial for any business seeking to thrive. As we delve into "KPIs for AI Success," it becomes clear that determining the right key performance indicators (KPIs) involves more than just numbers—it encapsulates a holistic appraisal of both tangible and intangible benefits AI can deliver.

KPIs play a vital role in bridging the gap between AI's complex capabilities and business leaders' expectations. They provide a concrete set of metrics that help assess whether AI implementations are aligning with overarching business objectives. For instance, an AI-driven customer service chat system may be evaluated not only for response accuracy but also for its impact on customer satisfaction and cost efficiency.

One foundational KPI category includes operational efficiency metrics. By measuring aspects such as the reduction in time spent on routine tasks and error rate improvement, businesses can tangibly assess AI's ability to streamline operations. These metrics highlight how effectively AI is reshaping workflows and improving productivity, directly impacting the organization's bottom line.

In parallel, customer-related KPIs are critical in illuminating AI's influence on user engagement and satisfaction. Metrics such as Net Promoter Score (NPS), customer retention rates, and service response time offer insights into how AI-driven solutions are enhancing customer experiences. Positive shifts in these KPIs are strong indicators of AI's role in fostering loyalty and driving revenue growth.

Beyond operational and customer metrics, innovation is a key area where AI's influence can be measured. Successful AI implementations often lead to new products, services, or business models. Tracking the rate of product development or the introduction of AI-enhanced features can serve as a KPI, reflecting AI's contribution to an organization's innovative capacity. This approach ensures that AI is not only optimizing existing processes but is also a catalyst for strategic growth.

Financial performance metrics should not be overlooked. The return on investment (ROI) from AI initiatives remains a pivotal KPI for business decision-makers. Calculating ROI involves assessing the financial gains derived from AI applications against the costs incurred during implementation. This KPI aids in determining the overall profitability and sustainability of AI projects.

While quantitative KPIs are essential, qualitative metrics hold significant value in comprehensively understanding AI's impact. Employee sentiment and adoption rates can signal the degree to which AI solutions are being embraced within an organization. These metrics shed light on workforce readiness and cultural adaptability, both critical for the sustained success of AI initiatives.

Furthermore, it is advantageous to have KPIs that track AI model performance directly. Metrics such as precision, recall, and F1 score are instrumental in evaluating the efficacy of machine learning models. These KPIs ensure that the AI systems not only meet technical benchmarks but also adapt to evolving datasets over time, maintaining accuracy and reliability.

Ethical considerations, frequently highlighted due to AI's pervasive impact, can also be monitored through specific KPIs. These may include metrics related to bias and fairness, assessing the extent to which AI systems adhere to ethical guidelines and regulatory standards. This is particularly important as businesses strive to maintain trust and integrity in AI deployments.

The effectiveness of AI must ultimately be seen through the lens of strategic alignment. KPIs should be designed to reflect AI's role in achieving strategic business objectives, whether it's penetrating new markets, enhancing competitive differentiation, or driving sustainable practices. Success in this regard is often measured by leadership teams in relation to long-term vision and mission objectives.

As businesses navigate the complexities of AI, establishing a robust KPI framework involves collaboration across departments, ensuring cross-functional buy-in and a shared understanding of AI's potential and limitations. It is this cohesive approach that transforms KPIs from mere statistical tools into strategic instruments for orchestrating AI success.

In sum, defining and using the right KPIs is intrinsic to measuring AI success and maximizing its impact. For business leaders, this means prioritizing KPIs that align with strategic objectives and considering a diverse set of metrics that encompass performance, innovation, customer satisfaction, and ethical usage. Doing so not only gauges the present effectiveness of AI initiatives but also sets the stage for continuous improvement and sustained competitive advantage.

Analyzing ROI from AI Implementations

As businesses increasingly integrate artificial intelligence into their operations, understanding the return on investment (ROI) is essential. The allure of AI lies not just in its technological prowess, but in its potential to deliver tangible financial benefits. However, unpacking these benefits and quantifying them requires a holistic approach that goes beyond mere numbers.

When measuring ROI from AI implementations, companies must examine both direct and indirect impacts. Direct impacts often include measurable factors like cost savings, revenue increases, and operational efficiencies. For instance, automating routine tasks can significantly reduce labor costs, while predictive analytics can boost sales by enhancing customer targeting. These immediate gains are tempting to showcase AI's effectiveness.

But the true value of AI often lies in its indirect benefits, which can be harder to quantify. These might encompass improved customer satisfaction, better decision-making capabilities, and increased innovation within the organization. Enhanced customer satisfaction, for example, can lead to increased loyalty and repeat business, which, though indirect, ultimately impacts the bottom line.

Another crucial aspect of analyzing AI ROI involves time horizons. While some benefits, like cost reductions, may materialize quickly, others, such as strategic adaptability and market positioning, require a longer-term perspective. AI implementations often involve initial investments and a learning curve; hence, patience and strategic foresight are key.

Understanding the ROI of AI also calls for rigorous evaluation frameworks. Businesses need a firm grasp of KPIs tailored to their specific AI initiatives. These KPIs should reflect both quantitative metrics, such as performance improvements and qualitative impacts, such as employee engagement and innovation rates. The challenge is ensuring these KPIs align with the overall business objectives, making the connection between AI implementations and business goals crystal clear.

Selecting the right AI use cases plays a pivotal role in maximizing ROI. Companies should prioritize AI applications that align closely with their strategic priorities and possess a clear path to value creation. Not every process will benefit equally from AI, and identifying the areas with the highest potential ROI is crucial for success.

The story of AI ROI wouldn't be complete without acknowledging the organizational changes AI entails. It can transform workflows, require new skills, and alter traditional business models. These transformations bring their own costs and benefits, complicating ROI calculations but also offering opportunities for deeper value creation and competitive advantage.

One effective strategy to gauge AI ROI is through pilot projects. Running pilots can provide invaluable insights into the potential financial and operational impacts of AI before a full-scale rollout. They offer a chance to learn, iterate, and refine AI solutions, ensuring the maximum return once implemented at scale.

Additionally, businesses need to be cautious about overestimating ROI due to technological optimism. AI, while powerful, isn't a magic bullet. It requires careful planning, execution, and ongoing management to truly deliver on its promises. Having realistic expectations and clear strategies for overcoming implementation challenges is essential for capturing significant ROI.

In conclusion, analyzing ROI from AI implementations demands a nuanced understanding of both quantitative and qualitative impacts. Companies must look beyond immediate financial gains and consider long-term strategic benefits. By carefully evaluating the alignment of AI applications with business objectives and ensuring the right organizational changes accompany technological ones, businesses can unlock the profound potential of AI and reap substantial ROI.

Chapter 20:
Real-World AI Case Studies

In this chapter, we delve into compelling real-world examples that demonstrate how AI is transforming industries and redefining business success. From retail giants leveraging AI for personalized customer experiences to financial institutions using machine learning for fraud detection and risk management, these case studies illustrate the profound impact of AI when strategically integrated into business models. Manufacturing sectors are witnessing enhanced efficiency as AI predicts maintenance needs, while healthcare providers use AI-driven analytics to improve patient outcomes. These stories not only highlight successful AI adoption but also offer invaluable insights into the strategies employed by industry leaders to overcome challenges and drive innovation. By understanding these real-world applications, business leaders can glean actionable lessons that inform their own AI strategies, positioning their organizations for success in an increasingly competitive landscape. These case studies are a testament to AI's potential to unlock unprecedented opportunities and advantages when aligned with clear business objectives and informed leadership.

Successful AI Adoption Stories

Successful AI adoption doesn't occur overnight. It's a journey marked by strategic foresight, organizational alignment, and iterative learning. Many companies have embarked on this transformative path, ultimately reaping substantial benefits. Among them, several standout

136

stories illuminate the diverse applications and tangible outcomes of integrating AI into business operations.

Consider the case of a leading retail giant that harnessed the power of machine learning to revolutionize its inventory management. This company faced a persistent challenge: balancing stock levels to meet customer demand without overstocking or wasting resources. By implementing AI-driven predictive analytics, the retailer was able to analyze historical sales data, seasonal trends, and real-time factors affecting purchase behavior. This predictive power transformed their inventory system, significantly reducing waste and out-of-stock situations. As a result, customer satisfaction improved alongside a notable increase in sales, setting a precedent for the retail sector.

In the financial services industry, AI's impact has been equally profound. A global bank, for instance, sought to enhance its fraud detection system. In the past, the bank relied on traditional methods that often flagged legitimate transactions as fraudulent, a costly inconvenience for customers. By adopting an AI-based solution that used deep learning algorithms, the bank effectively reduced false positives while detecting sophisticated fraudulent patterns more swiftly. This streamlined process not only curbed financial losses but also bolstered trust and loyalty among its clients.

AI has also proven essential in the realm of customer service. A telecommunications company, facing high customer churn rates, turned to AI to improve its customer experience. By deploying AI-powered chatbots and virtual assistants, it was able to offer 24/7 support, answer inquiries in multiple languages, and deliver personalized recommendations based on user behavior. This round-the-clock service transformed customer interactions, driving up satisfaction scores and reducing churn, which, in turn, enhanced revenue stability.

Meanwhile, in the manufacturing sector, an AI-powered predictive maintenance system enabled an aerospace company to push the boundaries of operational efficiency. By integrating AI with IoT sensors on machinery, the company could predict potential equipment failures before they occurred. This foresight allowed for timely interventions, minimizing downtime and operational disruptions. The cost savings were substantial, but more importantly, the company achieved greater reliability and trust in its production capabilities, essential in a highly competitive market.

The healthcare industry offers another inspiring example of AI adoption. A hospital network integrated AI to streamline its administrative and clinical processes. By utilizing natural language processing and machine learning, the hospital automated patient records management, making it easier for doctors to access comprehensive and up-to-date information. Moreover, AI-assisted imaging tools improved diagnostic accuracy and speed, particularly in radiology, where the technology identified anomalies with greater precision than traditional methods. These advancements resulted in not only improved patient outcomes but also enhanced operational efficiencies.

Another intriguing case is in the transport sector, where an AI-enabled logistics solution helped a shipping company optimize its routing and scheduling. AI algorithms processed vast datasets on traffic, weather conditions, and delivery priorities to devise optimal routes. This efficiency led to diminished fuel consumption, reduced emissions, and faster delivery times, aligning the company's objectives with sustainability goals while maintaining competitive service levels.

Even smaller enterprises have realized AI's transformative potential. A regional food distributor lacking extensive resources adopted AI for demand forecasting. Leveraging cloud-based AI tools, the company integrated AI into its supply chain, predicting demand fluctuations with considerable accuracy. This strategic advantage enabled the distributor to outpace competitors, expand its market presence, and remain resilient in volatile market conditions.

Technological innovation through AI is not limited to product-centric enterprises. A consulting firm specializing in market research employed AI to automate data collection and analysis. This led to delivering insights at an unprecedented speed, freeing up analysts to focus on strategic tasks and strengthening the firm's value proposition to its clients. This integration of AI has exemplified how service-based industries can harness technology for operational excellence.

Not to be overlooked, AI's role in driving corporate strategy is pivotal. A multinational corporation incorporated AI tools to sift through complex datasets, informing its strategic planning with precision analytics that were previously unattainable. This approach provided the company with a competitive edge, allowing leaders to make well-informed decisions in real time, signaling a shift from reactive to proactive strategic management.

The public sector has its own success stories. A government agency focused on urban planning utilized AI to enhance city resource allocation and energy management. By analyzing patterns in electricity consumption, traffic flows, and water usage, AI-driven solutions facilitated better planning and resource distribution, leading to more sustainable urban environments. Citizens benefited from improved public services, exemplifying AI's potential to enhance societal well-being.

Successful AI adoption isn't tied to a single approach or industry; it's the result of aligning innovative technology with specific business goals and nurturing an organizational culture willing to embrace change. The narratives presented here are just the beginning. These stories highlight the potential to rethink conventional business models, streamline operations, and redefine competitive landscapes. As seen, the impact of AI is multifaceted and transformative, underscoring the imperative for leaders across all sectors to consider how they might harness this powerful technology to drive success in their own organizations.

As we explore these successful implementations, it's essential to recognize that while the potential benefits of AI are immense, the journey is fraught with challenges. The organizations that thrive are those that approach AI adoption with careful planning, adaptability, and an unwavering focus on value creation. Thus, ushering in an era where intelligence, both artificial and human, coexist to foster unprecedented advancements and opportunities.

Learning from Industry Leaders

In every industry, the leaders who embrace innovation often define the future. This couldn't be truer for the rapidly evolving domain of Artificial Intelligence (AI). By examining how these trailblazers have implemented AI to revolutionize their industries, business leaders everywhere can glean invaluable insights. These real-world lessons aren't just academic—they're a roadmap for anyone eager to drive transformation and unlock the full potential of AI in their own organizations.

Consider the transformative journey of Amazon. From its humble beginnings as an online bookstore, Amazon has harnessed AI to redefine not just retail, but logistics and cloud computing. By leveraging machine learning algorithms, they've optimized their supply chain to be one of the most efficient globally, ensuring that a vast array of products reaches customers in record time. Their recommendation engine, powered by AI, offers personalized shopping experiences, significantly boosting sales. For business leaders, Amazon's approach highlights the importance of integrating AI into core operations and customer interactions, paving the way for efficiency and enhanced customer satisfaction.

Next, look at the strides made by Alphabet's Google. Their strategic use of AI isn't limited to their well-known search engine. Google's DeepMind has been at the forefront of machine learning and neural networks, achieving breakthroughs like AlphaGo, which surpassed human capabilities in the complex game of Go. This achievement wasn't just a milestone for gaming; it illuminated the potential for AI in solving intricate problems across diverse sectors. Google's prowess demonstrates that investing in foundational AI research can yield tools and systems with applications far beyond their initial scope, creating opportunities that few could have anticipated.

The automotive industry provides another compelling example. Tesla, under Elon Musk's leadership, has seamlessly integrated AI to push the boundaries of autonomous driving. By equipping their vehicles with extensive sensor suites and real-time processing capabilities, Tesla has developed advanced driver assistance systems. These systems not only enhance safety but also pave the way for fully autonomous vehicles. For industries reliant on logistics and transportation, Tesla teaches that the future isn't merely about adopting AI—it's about embedding it into the very fabric of product and service design.

In the financial services sector, Goldman Sachs has redefined decision-making through AI adoption. By implementing machine learning algorithms, they predict market trends with unparalleled accuracy, manage risk more effectively, and tailor services to individual clients. Through AI, they have transformed vast datasets into actionable insights, offering a level of customization and foresight previously unimaginable. Such cases illustrate the transformative power of AI in financial analysis and strategic foresight, urging leaders to embrace data-driven decision-making.

Healthcare, too, is benefitting from AI's potential. IBM Watson's journey showcases how AI can revolutionize diagnostics and treatment options. Watson's ability to process vast databases of medical literature allows it to assist physicians in making more informed decisions, offering tailored treatments to patients. While challenges remain in data standardization and integration, IBM's efforts demonstrate the promise of AI to not just enhance human capabilities but extend lives by improving healthcare outcomes.

AI isn't limited to large corporations; it's also transforming industries like agriculture. John Deere, an agricultural behemoth, has adopted AI to improve crop yields through precision agriculture. By using sensors, IoT devices, and machine learning, they provide farmers with insights for optimizing planting and harvesting. This approach maximizes productivity while minimizing resource use. The lesson here for businesses in resource-dependent industries is clear: AI can optimize operations, reduce waste, and enhance sustainability.

. AI's scope is also reshaping customer service across multiple industries. Consider the use of chatbots and virtual assistants in companies like Bank of America and Starbucks. These AI tools answer customer queries in real-time, ensuring a seamless customer experience while allowing companies to gather and analyze user data. Such data-driven insights help in designing more intuitive and personalized services, reinforcing the importance of customer-centric AI applications in maintaining competitive edge.

The aviation industry provides another fascinating application of AI through companies like Boeing and Airbus. They employ AI for predictive maintenance, analyzing data from thousands of sensors on aircraft to foresee equipment failures before they occur. This proactive approach ensures safety, reduces delays, and cuts maintenance costs. For leaders in manufacturing or industries where machinery is integral, predictive maintenance powered by AI is a lesson in preventing costly disruptions and enhancing operational efficiency.

Moreover, Unilever, in the consumer goods sector, exemplifies the use of AI for enhancing consumer insights and optimizing supply chains. They use AI-driven analytics to better understand consumer preferences and behaviors, allowing them to tailor products and marketing strategies more effectively. Unilever's approach illustrates how AI can drive market relevance and consumer satisfaction, emphasizing the role of data in aligning business strategies with customer needs.

While these industry giants illuminate AI's transformative potential, their journeys underscore a vital principle for all business leaders: successful AI implementation is often iterative. It requires a willingness to experiment, a commitment to employee training, and an infrastructure that supports data collection and analysis. Moreover, fostering a culture that values innovation and embraces change is imperative.

It's also crucial to acknowledge the ethical considerations these pioneers face. Balancing innovation with responsibility, addressing data privacy concerns, and mitigating AI biases remain significant challenges. Industry leaders who've managed to maintain trust while pushing the boundaries of AI provide a blueprint for ethically navigating the AI landscape.

In conclusion, learning from these industry frontrunners offers a multitude of strategies and lessons, but it's not about imitation. Instead, it's about adaptation—taking inspiration from their successes and challenges to carve out unique paths tailored to specific organizational needs and market conditions. By understanding the broader context and potential of AI, business leaders can not only stay competitive but drive their industries towards a more innovative and efficient future.

Chapter 21:
AI in Small and Medium Enterprises

There's an undeniable wave of transformation rippling through small and medium enterprises (SMEs) as they embrace Artificial Intelligence (AI) to carve out new efficiencies and competitive edges. AI isn't just for the tech giants anymore; it's leveling the playing field for businesses ready to seize opportunities that were previously out of reach. By leveraging AI's capabilities, SMEs can optimize operations, enhance customer experiences, and unlock insights buried within data that would otherwise remain untapped. Tailored AI solutions allow these businesses to automate mundane tasks, freeing up valuable resources to focus on innovation and growth. As SMEs incorporate AI into their strategies, they're equipped not just to survive in an increasingly complex marketplace, but to thrive by harnessing the power of intelligent technology that's as adaptable and driven as they are.

Opportunities for SMEs with AI

Small and Medium Enterprises (SMEs) play a crucial role in the global economy. They're often hailed as the backbone of many economies, driving innovation, providing employment, and contributing significantly to GDP. For these businesses, embracing AI isn't just a choice—it's increasingly a necessity to stay competitive. The agile nature of SMEs gives them a unique ability to rapidly adapt AI technologies, offering a plethora of opportunities that larger companies might struggle to realize due to their size and bureaucratic processes.

One key opportunity AI presents for SMEs is the ability to streamline and optimize operations. AI algorithms can handle repetitive tasks that typically consume a lot of time and resources, allowing employees to focus on more strategic, creative aspects of their roles. For instance, inventory management, often a complex juggling act for SMEs, can be significantly improved using AI-driven forecasting models. These models can assess past sales data, understand market trends, and predict future demand with remarkable accuracy, minimizing both overstock and stockouts.

Moreover, AI offers a game-changing potential in customer relationship management. SMEs often pride themselves on personalized, high-touch customer service. AI can take this a step further by providing insights into customer behavior and preferences. Machine learning algorithms can analyze purchase histories, online behaviors, and even social media interactions to provide a nuanced understanding of each customer's needs. Armed with this information, SMEs can tailor their marketing efforts to offer personalized recommendations, improving customer satisfaction and loyalty.

Another significant opportunity lies in enhancing decision-making processes. Decision-making in SMEs often happens faster and relies on fewer layers of bureaucracy than in larger corporations. By integrating AI into these processes, SMEs can leverage data-driven insights, transforming intuition-based decisions into informed, analytics-based strategies. For instance, predictive analytics can help identify emerging market trends, allowing SMEs to pivot or adapt their strategies proactively. This agility can be a significant competitive advantage in rapidly changing markets.

Furthermore, AI technology can help SMEs improve their cybersecurity posture, an area that's often under-prioritized due to resource constraints. AI systems can monitor networks continuously, identifying anomalies or potential security breaches in real time. This capability helps in preemptively addressing threats before they can inflict damage, thus safeguarding critical business data and maintaining customer trust.

One of the most appealing aspects of AI for SMEs is its potential to level the playing field in terms of market access and competitive capability. Advanced technologies that were once the privilege of large enterprises are now becoming accessible to SMEs, thanks to cloud-based AI services. These services lower the barriers of entry, allowing smaller businesses to access and deploy AI tools without the need for substantial upfront investments in infrastructure.

Additionally, AI can play a transformative role in product development and innovation. By analyzing large datasets, AI can identify gaps in the market or inspire novel features that resonate with customer desires. For example, a small tech company could use AI-driven analytics to study user feedback and usage patterns, leading to the development of new product features that are directly aligned with user needs.

Talent acquisition is another area where AI holds substantial promise. SMEs, often with limited HR resources, can deploy AI-driven recruitment tools to screen applications and identify top candidates. These tools can automate initial screening processes, analyze candidates' qualifications and experience, and even predict a candidate's future job performance based on existing data patterns. This not only streamlines the hiring process but also helps ensure a better match between employee roles and candidates, enhancing productivity and reducing turnover.

Despite these opportunities, it's important for SMEs to prioritize a strategic approach toward AI implementation. The technology itself is not a magic bullet. Success with AI comes from aligning its capabilities with clear business objectives and understanding where it can deliver the most value. SMEs need to be wary of overextending resources, attempting to integrate AI into areas where it may not yet be ready to produce tangible benefits.

To fully leverage AI, SMEs should consider upskilling their workforce or hiring necessary AI talent. Understanding the basics of AI and data analytics can empower teams to utilize these tools more effectively. Moreover, fostering a culture that embraces technology and encourages experimentation allows SMEs to be more agile and innovative in their application of AI.

In conclusion, AI offers a plethora of opportunities for SMEs to enhance efficiency, improve customer relationships, optimize decision-making, and secure their operations. By strategically implementing AI, SMEs can not only remain competitive but also thrive in a tech-driven marketplace. While challenges may exist, the potential benefits of integrating AI into SME operations far outweigh the hurdles, paving the way for a more innovative and responsive business landscape.

Tailoring AI Solutions for Smaller Businesses

In the competitive landscape of today's business world, smaller enterprises often find themselves at a crossroads: harnessing cutting-edge technology without the resources of their larger counterparts. Yet, this challenge presents an exciting opportunity. Tailoring AI solutions specifically for small and medium enterprises (SMEs) is not only feasible but can significantly democratize the advantages of AI. By focusing on customized strategies, SMEs can transform their operations and drive substantial growth.

AI's potential is immense, yet its deployment must be strategic, especially for businesses operating with tight budgets and limited expertise. The first step lies in understanding the specific needs of the enterprise. What are the pain points or areas ripe for improvement? Identifying these is crucial because AI isn't a one-size-fits-all approach. Instead, it's about leveraging technology to address distinct challenges. For smaller businesses, these might range from improving customer service to streamlining inventory management.

Many SMEs mistakenly believe that AI implementation demands significant upfront investments, both financially and technologically. This perception can deter businesses from even exploring AI's potential. However, the rapid evolution of AI has led to the development of cost-effective solutions. Cloud-based platforms, for example, offer subscription models that are scalable, allowing SMEs to pay only for what they use, which is a game changer in cost management.

Moreover, many AI tools today are designed with user-friendliness in mind. SMEs don't necessarily need a dedicated team of data scientists to deploy AI effectively. Thanks to intuitive interfaces and comprehensive support systems provided by AI vendors, businesses can embark on their AI journey with relative ease. Additionally, the growing sector of AI consulting services tailored for small businesses can bridge knowledge gaps, ensuring that the technology is implemented correctly and effectively.

Next, consider the importance of feasibility and integration. Any AI solution for SMEs should seamlessly integrate with existing systems. This minimizes disruption and helps maintain operational flow. SMEs should prioritize AI tools that offer robust APIs or plug-in capabilities. Such features ensure that AI enhancements complement rather than complicate current workflows, effectively streamlining processes.

Strategically, it's crucial for SMEs to take a phased approach to AI implementation. Starting small with pilot projects can yield significant insights. This allows for testing and refinement without overwhelming the organization. By analyzing these smaller-scale implementations,

SMEs can better understand the impact and potential adjustments needed before wider application. This cautious but deliberate approach helps cultivate an AI-ready environment and mitigates risks.

Cultural readiness is another aspect SMEs must tackle. For AI initiatives to succeed, internal stakeholders must embrace change. This means educating teams about AI's benefits and involve them in the transition process. It's not just about integrating technology but fostering a mindset open to innovation. Leaders within the organization play a vital role in championing these initiatives, setting the tone and pace for adoption.

When considering AI tools, it's also essential for SMEs to evaluate the data they have. AI's effectiveness is largely dependent on the quality of data fed into it. SMEs should invest in establishing clean, structured data collection practices before implementing AI. Small businesses can enhance their outcomes by ensuring that the data is accurate and representative of their operational realities.

The agility of SMEs offers a unique advantage over larger enterprises. Without the burdens of legacy systems or complex hierarchies, smaller businesses can pivot quickly, adapting AI solutions to changing business landscapes. This flexibility is paramount as AI tools themselves continue to evolve, ensuring sustained competitive advantage and continuous improvement.

To harness AI effectively, SMEs mustn't shy away from collaboration. Whether it's through partnerships with tech firms, joining industry consortiums, or collaborating with academic institutions, such alliances can provide access to advanced technologies and AI expertise. Not only do these partnerships offer financial relief, but they also bolster the skills and knowledge within the enterprise itself.

The role of government and industry bodies should not be overlooked. Many countries offer grants, tax incentives, or support programs specifically aimed at encouraging AI adoption within smaller businesses. SMEs should actively seek out these opportunities to lessen the financial burden and enhance their capabilities. Staying informed about these resources can provide a competitive edge.

Finally, success in tailoring AI solutions for smaller businesses requires an ongoing commitment to learning and adaptation. The world of AI is dynamic, with tools and best practices continually evolving. SMEs must remain proactive, updating their systems and knowledge base to ensure they are leveraging AI technologies to their fullest potential. In doing so, they position themselves not just as competitors in their markets, but as leaders in innovation.

By addressing these aspects, small and medium enterprises can turn the AI challenge into a compelling strategic opportunity. Tailoring AI solutions effectively allows SMEs to capitalize on technological advancements and reimagine what's possible within their spheres of influence, ultimately ensuring they don't just survive but thrive in the digital age.

Chapter 22:
Building Trust in AI Systems

Building trust in AI systems is paramount for businesses aiming to integrate these technologies seamlessly into their operations. At its core, trust hinges on transparency and explainability, crucial elements that allow stakeholders to understand and believe in AI-driven insights. For business leaders, the challenge is not just in deploying AI, but in ensuring it acts with both predictability and clarity. This means that users can confidently rely on AI systems to enhance decisions without fearing unintended consequences. As organizations strive for strategic advantages, crafting clear guidelines on data usage and algorithm fairness becomes non-negotiable. Such measures, coupled with ongoing education and communication, empower employees and customers alike to engage with AI confidently, fostering an environment where AI serves as a trusted partner rather than an enigmatic force. Trust, after all, is not the final step, but the foundation upon which sustainable AI success is built.

Transparency and Explainability

In the rapidly evolving world of Artificial Intelligence, transparency and explainability stand out as critical components for building trust in AI systems. As businesses integrate AI into their decision-making processes, it's essential to demystify these systems for users, stakeholders, and even regulators. For leaders aiming to harness the strategic advantages of AI, these elements are not just technical requirements but foundational to their adoption and long-term success.

Imagine if a critical decision in your company was made by an AI system that you couldn't comprehend or explain. It wouldn't be just unsettling; it could pose risks to your business operations and stakeholder relations. Transparency in AI hinges on how open and clear developers and organizations are about the algorithms used, the data processed, and the decisions made by these systems. It's about laying bare the working mechanism of AI in a way that aligns with organizational goals and user expectations.

Explainability goes hand in hand with transparency. While transparency may provide the technical details of how an AI system functions, explainability focuses on making these details understandable to non-experts. It's about translating complex algorithms into insights that business leaders can easily digest and use for strategic planning. This is crucial in bridging the gap between AI and human decision-makers, thereby fostering a culture of collaboration between technology and its users.

There are practical techniques to improve the explainability of AI models. One approach is developing interpretable models, which are inherently easier to understand. Techniques like decision trees and rule-based systems, though not as powerful as deep learning models, offer a visual representation of decision-making paths. Another approach involves simplifying complex models post hoc, using methods like LIME (Local Interpretable Model-agnostic Explanations) or SHAP (Shapley Additive exPlanations), which help in elucidating black-box models.

For leaders, advocating for and implementing transparency and explainability can lead to significant benefits. First, it enhances user confidence. Users are more likely to trust an AI system if they understand how it operates and how decisions are made. This is especially important in customer-facing applications, where opaque systems can result in user frustration and attrition.

Furthermore, transparency and explainability can mitigate bias in AI. When businesses openly scrutinize how their AI systems work, they can identify and address biases that might exist in the algorithm or data. This proactive approach not only ensures ethical AI deployment but also protects the organization from potential legal and reputational risks. After all, an unbiased AI system is a fair system—one that upholds the company's commitment to equality and fairness.

Regulations around AI are also tightening globally, and companies need to be prepared. Compliance with these regulations often requires demonstrating a high level of transparency and explainability in AI systems. Being ahead of this curve can position businesses not only in favorable regulatory standings but also as leaders in responsible AI deployment. This pursuit of transparency isn't just about avoiding penalties; it's about setting a benchmark in the industry for ethical and transparent AI implementation.

Business professionals playing a crucial role in decision-making processes must champion the move towards transparent and explainable AI. This means questioning AI vendors about the interpretability of their models, investing in training the workforce to understand AI outputs, and fostering a culture where technology and its processes are discussed openly. By doing so, businesses can effectively integrate AI into their strategic framework and maintain a competitive edge.

Of course, a fine balance must be struck to protect proprietary algorithms while still offering sufficient transparency to stakeholders. Businesses need to navigate this tension carefully, ensuring they provide enough information to satisfy the need for explainability without compromising their competitive advantages. This effort requires strategic thinking and an understanding of both technological and business landscapes.

In conclusion, transparency and explainability are more than just buzzwords in the AI community. They are essential variables in the equation of trust, shaping how AI technologies are received and utilized within organizations. As we move towards a future where AI permeates every aspect of business, these concepts will only grow in significance, demanding continuous investment and innovation from companies that aspire not only to adopt AI but also to lead the charge towards a transparent, explainable, and ultimately trustworthy AI era.

Building User Confidence

Building trust in AI systems is not a mere technical exercise; it's a critical business imperative. The success of AI in any organization hinges not only on its technical capabilities but also on the confidence users place in these systems. Confidence is cultivated through a comprehensive understanding of how AI systems operate, why they make certain decisions, and how they align with business objectives. It's about demystifying AI to foster a sense of empowerment among users, allowing them to integrate AI tools seamlessly into their workflows.

First and foremost, transparency is essential in fostering user confidence. Users want to know that AI systems are not 'black boxes'—impenetrable entities that churn out decisions without logic or explanation. Ensuring transparency involves providing clear, comprehensible insights into how AI models function and deliver results. This might entail offering detailed yet accessible documentation of AI algorithms, illustrating input-output relationships, and demonstrating how these processes tie into business strategy.

However, transparency alone isn't enough. Explainability complements transparency by going a step further. While transparency reveals what is happening, explainability covers why it is happening. AI systems should be able to account for their decisions, providing reasons that are understandable to the human mind. By doing so, organizations equip users with the knowledge to make informed decisions based on AI outputs, increasing their willingness to rely on these systems.

Building on explainability, an inclusive design process can further boost user confidence. When designing AI solutions, incorporating diverse perspectives ensures that the system resonates with a wide user base. By involving users early and often in the design process, from brainstorming to prototyping, organizations can create AI systems that users find intuitive and trustworthy. This participatory approach engenders a sense of ownership, where users feel as though the system was built with their needs and perspectives in mind.

Education and training play pivotal roles in further bolstering user confidence. As much as AI technology should adapt to human needs, users should also enhance their understanding of AI. Structured training programs can help demystify AI concepts, making users more comfortable and proficient in interacting with AI tools. Offering these programs can turn skepticism into trust, as users begin to appreciate the wide applicability and potential of AI in their routines.

Additionally, the role of leadership cannot be overstated in this context. Leaders set the tone for AI integration and use across their organizations. When leaders embrace AI and consistently highlight its successes and benefits, they contribute to building a culture of confidence. Their endorsement can remove skepticism and encourage teams to view AI as a tool for empowerment rather than replacement.

Creating a feedback loop between users and developers is another vital component. It facilitates continuous improvement while ensuring that the AI system remains aligned with user needs and expectations. By regularly reviewing and acting upon user feedback, organizations can refine AI systems, addressing any concerns and enhancing usability. This dynamic interaction between feedback and system improvement reassures users that their input is valued and integral to the system's evolution.

Moreover, reliable performance is a non-negotiable aspect of building confidence. Users must trust that AI systems will perform accurately and efficiently, without unpredictable failures. Rigorous testing and validation processes can assure the reliability of AI systems. By maintaining high performance standards across real-world scenarios, organizations can alleviate potential trust issues and enhance user willingness to engage with AI tools.

Addressing concerns around data privacy and security is also fundamental. Users are much more likely to trust AI systems if they're confident that their data is handled responsibly and ethically. Ensuring robust data protection measures and being transparent about data usage can mitigate fears regarding data breaches and misuse. Maintaining privacy by design principles further fosters a protective environment that builds user trust.

Ultimately, user confidence is a journey rather than a destination. It requires continuous effort, communication, and adaptation to meet evolving user needs. In crafting trust, organizations lay the groundwork for a successful AI deployment that translates technological advancements into tangible business value. By proactively addressing user confidence, businesses can leverage AI as a powerful partner in their strategic growth.

Chapter 23:
Cross-Industry AI Applications

Artificial Intelligence is breaking down the barriers between industries, creating a tech-driven symbiosis that reshapes traditional business landscapes. From healthcare to retail and e-commerce, AI's adaptability and transformative power are profoundly evident. In healthcare, AI empowers personalized medicine, augments diagnostic precision, and automates administrative tasks, enhancing patient outcomes while optimizing operational efficiency. Meanwhile, in retail and e-commerce, AI redefines customer experience by leveraging predictive analytics for inventory management, personalized shopping experiences, and dynamic pricing strategies. By integrating AI across industries, organizations not only streamline their processes but also unlock unprecedented levels of innovation and value creation. The fluidity with which AI applications traverse different sectors underscores its role as a universal catalyst for strategic advantage and sustainable growth. As business leaders explore these cross-industry opportunities, they foster a forward-thinking mindset necessary for navigating this new era of inter-industry collaboration and competitiveness.

AI in Healthcare

Artificial Intelligence is transforming the healthcare sector in profound ways, unleashing new potentials for improving patient outcomes, operational efficiency, and medical research. The impact of AI in healthcare is vast, touching everything from diagnosis and treatment planning to patient management and drug discovery. Businesses that operate within or alongside the healthcare sector have a unique opportunity to leverage AI technologies to drive significant advancements and efficiencies.

One of the most prominent applications of AI in healthcare is its role in diagnostic processes. AI algorithms, particularly those using deep learning techniques, have shown remarkable abilities in image recognition, often rivaling or even surpassing human experts in areas like radiology and pathology. By analyzing medical images, AI can assist in detecting diseases such as cancer at an early stage, where timely intervention can be life-saving. This doesn't just improve accuracy but also significantly reduces the time required for diagnosis, effectively tackling the bottlenecks in patient care processes.

Moreover, AI-powered diagnostic tools facilitate a more personalized approach to healthcare. By integrating data from various sources—such as genetic information, medical histories, and lifestyle factors—AI systems can develop patient-specific treatment plans. This personalized medicine ensures higher efficacy of treatments while minimizing potential side effects, ultimately enhancing the quality of care patients receive.

AI's ability to analyze vast amounts of data quickly and accurately makes it an invaluable tool in drug discovery and development. Traditional drug discovery processes are costly and time-intensive. AI algorithms can process biomedical data to identify potential drug candidates more swiftly, predict interactions, and determine efficacy before clinical trials. This accelerates the development timeline and reduces costs, enabling pharmaceutical companies to bring innovative treatments to market more efficiently.

Another critical area where AI is making strides is in the management of healthcare facilities. AI systems help optimize clinical operations, improve patient flow, and manage hospital staff more effectively. Predictive analytics can forecast patient admissions, ensuring adequate resource allocation and reducing waiting times. This efficiency not only improves patient satisfaction but also enhances the operational capabilities of healthcare institutions, ultimately leading to cost savings.

The integration of AI in healthcare also paves the way for enhanced patient monitoring. Wearable devices and IoT-enabled sensors collect real-time data on vital signs and other health metrics. AI algorithms analyze this data to detect deviations from normal patterns, providing early alerts for potential health issues. This continuous monitoring supports proactive care, particularly beneficial for managing chronic conditions.

Beyond clinical and operational applications, AI plays a vital role in administrative tasks within healthcare organizations. Automation of processes such as appointment scheduling, billing, and patient records management reduces administrative burdens, allowing healthcare professionals to focus more on patient care. By streamlining these processes, AI contributes to cost efficiency and improves overall service delivery.

AI's transformative potential also extends into healthcare research. Data mining and AI-driven analytics provide researchers with insights into complex diseases, uncovering new patterns and relationships. Such insights are crucial for understanding diseases and discovering novel therapeutic approaches. Furthermore, AI accelerates the research process by analyzing existing scientific literature, enabling researchers to stay abreast of the latest developments and integrate findings swiftly into their work.

Nevertheless, the integration of AI in healthcare does not come without challenges. Ethical considerations, data privacy, and security concerns remain paramount. AI systems rely on extensive datasets, which often contain sensitive health information. Ensuring robust data protection measures and transparent, ethical use of AI is essential to maintaining patient trust and complying with legal standards.

There's also the challenge of integrating AI technologies into existing healthcare systems. The complexity and diversity of systems across institutions require flexible AI solutions that can adapt and integrate seamlessly. Moreover, the workforce needs to be prepared to work alongside these advanced technologies, necessitating substantial training and a cultural shift within the industry.

Yet, the promise AI holds for healthcare can't be overstated. As the technology continues to evolve, its potential applications in healthcare will expand further, offering unprecedented opportunities to enhance patient care, streamline operations, and foster innovation. Business leaders and managers with a stake in healthcare can drive these advancements by strategically leveraging AI, ensuring their organizations remain at the forefront of innovation.

In conclusion, AI's role in healthcare represents a paradigm shift towards a more efficient, effective, and personalized approach to patient care. Embracing AI not only enhances competitive advantage but also propels the healthcare industry towards a future where technology and humanity intertwine seamlessly to deliver remarkable medical breakthroughs. By adopting AI strategically, the healthcare sector stands to make significant strides in improving the overall quality and accessibility of healthcare services worldwide.

AI in Retail and E-commerce

The fusion of artificial intelligence (AI) in retail and e-commerce has been nothing short of transformative. This industry has witnessed a profound evolution as businesses leverage AI to redefine customer engagement, streamline operations, and optimize supply chains. AI's role in retail and e-commerce isn't just about automation; it's about creating meaningful connections with customers and enhancing the shopping experience.

Retailers today are capitalizing on AI's ability to analyze enormous datasets to unearth insights that were once unreachable. This data-driven approach has revolutionized how businesses understand consumer behaviors, preferences, and trends. Machine learning algorithms process vast amounts of data to predict consumer needs before they even realize them. This predictive capability allows retailers to customize their offerings, ensuring the right products reach the right customers at precisely the right time.

One of the most prominent applications of AI in retail is in the realm of personalization. Personalization isn't just a buzzword; it's a critical driver of customer loyalty and revenue. Through AI, retailers create unique shopping experiences by tailoring recommendations to individual preferences. Algorithms analyze browsing history, purchase data, and even social media activity to provide personalized product suggestions. This level of curation not only satisfies customers but can significantly boost sales.

Dynamic pricing is another significant innovation powered by AI in retail and e-commerce. By constantly analyzing market trends, inventory levels, and competitor pricing, AI systems enable retailers to optimize their pricing strategies in real-time. This dynamic pricing ensures that businesses remain competitive while also maximizing profit margins, creating a harmonious balance that is often pivotal in today's volatile market conditions.

AI also plays a pivotal role in enhancing customer service through chatbots and virtual assistants. These AI-powered tools provide instant, around-the-clock support, addressing customer inquiries efficiently and reducing the burden on human agents. This not only leads to increased customer satisfaction but also allows human resources to focus on more complex tasks, thereby improving overall operational efficiency.

The integration of AI into inventory management has also been revolutionary. Retailers can optimize stock levels through AI-powered demand forecasting, reducing the incidences of overstocking or stockouts. This foresight is crucial, especially for businesses with large product catalogs, ensuring they maintain optimal inventory levels and reduce unnecessary costs.

Furthermore, AI technologies are enhancing visual search capabilities. This technology allows users to search for products using images rather than text, offering a more intuitive and engaging shopping experience. Visual search can break language barriers and is particularly beneficial for fashion and home decor retailers, where customer preference is often visually driven.

Fraud detection and prevention have also been significantly enhanced by AI applications in e-commerce. AI systems have the ability to detect unusual patterns in transaction data, alerting retailers to potential fraudulent activities instantly. This proactive approach helps in safeguarding both the consumer's financial information and the retailer's credibility.

Warehouse automation, powered by AI, has seen an escalation in efficiency and accuracy. Robots equipped with AI can manage inventory, pick and pack orders, and handle returns with precision and speed. This automation reduces human error, accelerates processes, and ultimately leads to faster delivery times, which is a massive competitive edge in e-commerce.

Embracing AI in retail and e-commerce also involves ethical considerations. Transparency in AI decisions, data privacy, and algorithmic bias are significant concerns that businesses must address. Building trust with customers through explainable AI practices is crucial. As retailers become more data-driven, ensuring ethical AI use will be vital in maintaining consumer trust and compliance with regulations.

As we look to the future, the potential of AI in retail and e-commerce remains vast and largely untapped. The industry stands on the brink of a new era where AI-driven innovations will continue to redefine how retailers interact with customers and operate internally. Retailers that can successfully integrate AI into their strategies will not only enhance their operational competencies but also cement their positions as leaders in an increasingly competitive marketplace.

In summary, AI's application in retail and e-commerce is an embodiment of technology's promise to transform industries. By adopting AI solutions, businesses can deliver superior customer experiences, operational excellence, and sustainable growth. The key lies in effectively integrating AI to not only meet but exceed evolving consumer expectations, thus maintaining relevance and fostering long-term success in the digital age.

Chapter 24:
Scaling AI Initiatives

Scaling AI initiatives across an organization requires a well-orchestrated strategy that aligns technological capabilities with business objectives. As companies look to expand AI across various business units, success hinges on the ability to integrate AI seamlessly into existing workflows while fostering a culture of continuous innovation. This involves not only deploying more robust AI systems but ensuring scalability through flexible architectures, sustainable investment, and a skilled workforce adept in AI technologies. A collaborative approach, where cross-functional teams share insights and best practices, facilitates broader acceptance and optimizes resource allocation. By prioritizing scalability, businesses can harness the full potential of AI to drive growth, maintain competitive advantage, and adapt to the evolving digital landscape, ensuring that AI initiatives are both impactful and enduring.

Expanding AI Across Business Units

Artificial Intelligence is not just a tool for a single department; rather, it's a transformative force that can reshape entire organizations. Imagine each business unit as a spoke on a wheel, where AI serves as the hub that brings coherence and efficiency to the whole system. Expanding AI across various business units requires more than technology—it demands a strategic approach that aligns with both organizational goals and unit-specific objectives.

The first step in expanding AI across business units involves understanding the unique needs and challenges of each unit. Take, for example, a marketing department that might aim to enhance customer engagement through personalized experiences, while the operations team could focus on optimizing supply chain logistics. Each unit will have its distinct requirements and expectations from AI solutions. Therefore, a one-size-fits-all approach won't suffice. Instead, tailored AI solutions should cater to the specific demands and strategic objectives of each business unit, ensuring that the implementation is both relevant and impactful.

It is crucial to foster a culture of collaboration and shared knowledge among different departments. When AI initiatives are siloed, the organization misses out on the synergistic benefits that can arise from cross-departmental insights and innovations. Encouraging open communication and knowledge sharing can break down the walls between departments. For instance, the insights gained from AI analytics in marketing can inform better resource allocation in operations, and vice versa. This collaborative culture ensures that the organization leverages AI to its full potential, deriving holistic benefits that extend beyond isolated gains.

Leadership plays a pivotal role in steering AI expansion efforts. Business leaders must champion the cause, not just by providing the necessary resources and technology but also by inspiring their teams to embrace AI-driven change. This involves setting a clear vision for AI integration and making strategic decisions that reflect an understanding of both technology and business dynamics. Leaders should act as facilitators who guide and support business units in navigating the complexities of AI adoption, ensuring that each unit remains aligned with the organization's overall objectives.

Investing in the right infrastructure is a non-negotiable component of scaling AI initiatives across business units. This means more than just acquiring advanced AI tools; it involves setting up a robust data ecosystem that ensures smooth data flow between departments. The infrastructure should be flexible enough to accommodate the varying demands of different business units, but unified to ensure consistency and quality in AI outputs. Reliable data pipelines, secure data storage, and efficient data processing are all key elements that support effective AI integration across the enterprise.

Additionally, empowering teams with the right skill sets can't be overlooked. Every business unit should be equipped with a talent pool that possesses both the technical know-how and a keen understanding of their functional domain. This could mean reskilling existing employees or hiring AI specialists who bring in fresh perspectives and advanced capabilities. Upskilling programs can be tailored to provide current employees with the tools they need to work alongside AI technologies, thus enhancing their roles rather than replacing them.

Measuring the impact of AI across business units can guide future strategy and investment. Key performance indicators (KPIs) specific to each business unit should be defined before AI implementation. These KPIs will differ across units; for example, in sales, KPIs might focus on lead conversion rates, while in HR, they could measure time-to-hire or employee engagement levels. Continuous monitoring of these metrics will not only demonstrate the value added by AI but also help refine processes and improve AI strategies over time.

Finally, it's essential to keep the end-users in focus. Every AI system or solution should ultimately serve the people using it—be it the employees in back-office functions or the customers interacting with your products and services. Ensuring that AI solutions are user-friendly and provide intuitive interfaces is crucial for widespread adoption. Feedback from end-users should be solicited regularly to drive iterative improvements and ensure that AI solutions remain relevant and effective.

To conclude, expanding AI across business units is a complex, yet rewarding endeavor that necessitates careful planning, strategic vision, and a commitment to continuous improvement. By aligning AI initiatives with specific business goals, fostering a culture of collaboration, investing in the right infrastructure, and empowering people with the right skills, organizations can unlock immense potential and drive transformative change across all levels.

Ensuring Scalability and Sustainability

Scaling AI initiatives isn't merely about expanding technical infrastructures or increasing data processing capabilities. It's about crafting a strategic framework that ensures long-term viability and adaptability within an ever-evolving technological landscape. Business leaders must adopt a holistic approach to scalability, recognizing that success depends on more than just the deployment of advanced algorithms or the integration of cutting-edge hardware. The real challenge lies in balancing rapid technological advancement with sustainable growth practices that align with the organization's core objectives and values.

To achieve scalability and sustainability, organizations need to embed flexibility and resilience into their AI strategies. Flexibility comes from designing systems that can accommodate new data sources and learn from shifts in market dynamics. Resilience, on the other hand, requires that these systems remain robust in the face of external shocks, such as regulatory changes or technological disruptions. By developing adaptive AI architectures, businesses can better respond to new opportunities and challenges, ensuring their AI initiatives remain impactful over time.

A critical aspect of ensuring scalability is the seamless integration of AI across various business units. This involves creating interconnected systems that facilitate the flow of information and insights between departments, enhancing synergy and collaboration. By breaking down silos and fostering a culture of shared learning, businesses can amplify the benefits of AI, driving innovation and efficiency across the organization. However, this integration is not without its challenges, particularly in larger organizations where existing processes and systems may not readily accommodate new technologies.

Investing in robust data management practices is foundational to sustainable AI scale. Data is the lifeblood of AI systems, and without secure, high-quality, and accessible data, even the most sophisticated algorithms can yield misleading results. Businesses need to implement comprehensive data governance frameworks that ensure data integrity and compliance with privacy regulations. This not only protects the organization against potential legal and ethical pitfalls but also enhances the trustworthiness of AI-driven insights.

Human capital plays a vital role in scaling AI sustainably. Organizations must cultivate AI literacy among their workforce, empowering employees to work effectively with AI systems and interpret their outputs accurately. This involves ongoing training and upskilling initiatives that keep pace with technological advancements and emerging industry trends. By nurturing a skilled workforce, companies can harness the full potential of AI and drive business growth while fostering a supportive and inclusive work environment.

Financial considerations also come into play when scaling AI initiatives. Effective budgeting and resource allocation are crucial to sustaining AI efforts over the long term. Business leaders must identify cost-effective AI solutions that align with their strategic objectives while ensuring that resources are distributed efficiently across projects. This requires a keen understanding of the cost-benefit dynamics of AI technologies and the ability to prioritize initiatives that offer the greatest return on investment.

The role of partnerships and collaborations cannot be overstated in the context of scalability and sustainability. By engaging with external stakeholders, such as technology providers, academic institutions, and industry consortia, businesses can access cutting-edge research and insights that drive innovation. Collaborative efforts also facilitate knowledge exchange and best practice sharing, enabling organizations to stay ahead of the curve in a rapidly changing AI landscape.

To ensure sustainability, ethical considerations must be integral to AI scaling strategies. Businesses must address issues of bias, transparency, and accountability, striving to develop AI systems that are fair, explainable, and free from unintended consequences. Adopting ethical AI practices not only safeguards the organization's reputation but also enhances the social acceptance and effectiveness of AI solutions. This requires a commitment to ongoing ethical evaluation and stakeholder engagement, fostering a dialogue around the responsible use of AI.

Finally, continuous innovation is essential to maintaining the scalability and sustainability of AI initiatives. Organizations must cultivate an innovation-driven culture that encourages experimentation and embraces change. This involves setting aside resources for research and development and creating an environment where new ideas are valued and promoted. By fostering a culture of innovation, businesses can ensure they remain at the forefront of AI technology, driving competitive advantage and business success in the long run.

In conclusion, ensuring scalability and sustainability in AI initiatives requires a multifaceted strategy that balances technical prowess with human and ethical considerations. Organizations that can seamlessly integrate AI into their operations, invest in data management and workforce development, and foster a culture of innovation and collaboration will be well-positioned to leverage AI for sustainable growth. As they navigate the complexities of scaling AI, business leaders must remain vigilant and adaptable, ready to pivot and evolve in response to new challenges and opportunities that the future holds.

Chapter 25:
AI and the Workforce of the Future

As AI reshapes industries, the workforce stands on the brink of a significant transformation, necessitating a proactive approach from business leaders. To harness AI's potential, organizations must anticipate shifts in employment landscapes, acknowledging both challenges and opportunities. As routine tasks become automated, the demand for roles emphasizing creativity, emotional intelligence, and complex problem-solving will surge. Thus, empowering employees through upskilling and reskilling initiatives isn't just beneficial—it's imperative. Forward-thinking leadership means investing in human capital and fostering a culture of continuous learning, ensuring that the synergy between man and machine thrives. By embracing these changes, companies not only secure their competitive edge but also cultivate a workforce resilient to the evolving demands of the AI-driven future.

Preparing for Changes in Employment

In an age where Artificial Intelligence (AI) is reshaping industries at an unprecedented pace, the workforce finds itself at a pivotal crossroads. The integration of AI into various job functions is not merely altering how tasks are completed; it's fundamentally redefining roles and responsibilities. The task for business leaders, managers, and professionals is to foresee and prepare for these changes in a way that benefits both their organizations and their employees. Understanding the evolving landscape and acting with intent is crucial for thriving in this new era of work.

The transition to an AI-driven workforce doesn't mean jobs will vanish overnight. Instead, we can expect a gradual shift where certain tasks are automated, and others are enhanced by technology. The key is identifying which roles are most susceptible to automation and which ones can leverage AI to augment human capabilities. For example, while AI can handle data analysis much faster than a human, it still requires the strategic oversight and decision-making skills that only people can provide.

Moreover, it's essential to recognize the new categories of jobs that will emerge as a result of AI advancements. Roles such as AI ethicists, data curators, and automation specialists are gaining prominence. These positions require skills that blend traditional knowledge with an understanding of advanced technology, presenting an opportunity for businesses to cultivate a workforce that's both diverse and adaptable. Emphasizing cross-disciplinary skills will become a significant competitive advantage.

One strategic approach to prepare for these changes is by fostering a culture of continuous learning within the organization. Upskilling and reskilling initiatives should not just be buzzwords, but integral parts of your corporate strategy. By investing in your workforce's education and training, you empower them to adapt to shifting demands and drive innovation. Encourage employees to pursue new learning opportunities, whether through online courses, workshops, or mentoring programs. This investment is often directly correlated with improved productivity and employee satisfaction.

Business implications of AI are vast and varied. As automation takes on more routine tasks, emphasis can shift to areas where human intuition and empathy shine, such as creative problem solving, strategic planning, and relationship management. Leaders must evaluate how AI can play a complementary role in these processes. AI is a tool to be leveraged, not a threat to be feared. Recognizing its potential to enhance rather than replace human work is a mindset shift necessary for future success.

However, preparing for changes in employment isn't just about focusing on skills and tasks. It demands a transformation in how organizations approach work itself. Flexible work environments and structures that allow for remote work, project-based assignments, and dynamic role definitions must be considered. This flexibility can help attract talent that is adaptable and eager to contribute to new initiatives. By modifying organizational structures to accommodate change, companies can remain agile and responsive to emerging trends and technologies.

Furthermore, it is crucial to communicate these changes effectively across the organization. Transparency regarding the impacts of AI on roles and responsibilities helps alleviate uncertainty and fear. Having open dialogues about how AI will influence their daily tasks and long-term opportunities assures employees that they are valued partners in this transformation. Regular feedback loops and change management strategies can aid in easing transitions and ensuring sustained engagement from the workforce.

Another vital component is ethical consideration in AI implementation. As new roles develop and technologies evolve, ensuring that ethical standards are maintained can prevent adverse outcomes that could harm the workforce and the organization's reputation. This implies prioritizing the creation of fair AI systems, guarding against biases, and securing employee data privacy. Ethical considerations should always be at the forefront, guiding AI strategies and implementation.

Finally, the impact of AI on employment can't be viewed in isolation. It forms part of a more extensive ecosystem involving societal shifts, economic conditions, and regulatory frameworks that also play a crucial role. Therefore, businesses must remain vigilant about these external factors that interact with their internal workforce strategies. Collaborating with industry partners, educational institutions, and government entities can provide valuable insights and assist in establishing comprehensive approaches tailored to specific industries.

In conclusion, preparing for changes in employment amidst AI's burgeoning presence requires a proactive and strategic mindset. This involves not only aligning business strategies with AI capabilities but also investing in the people who will drive these changes forward. As we stand on the precipice of a new era, the organizations that succeed will be those that view this transformation as an opportunity rather than a challenge. Harnessing AI's potential while nurturing and evolving the workforce will be the cornerstone of achieving lasting competitive advantage and innovation.

Upskilling and Reskilling Initiatives

As artificial intelligence (AI) reshapes industries and redefines traditional job roles, the importance of upskilling and reskilling initiatives has never been more critical. Business leaders today face the challenge of preparing their workforce for a future where technological fluency is as essential as any other skill. This challenge, however, also presents a significant opportunity to build a team that is agile, adaptable, and innovative. Companies must embrace a culture of continuous learning to stay ahead of the curve.

AI isn't just another tool; it's a transformative force that compels a reevaluation of existing skill sets. To harness the full potential of AI, employees must evolve. This evolution calls for targeted training programs that enable workers to acquire new skills relevant to AI-driven environments. For businesses, the key is to identify the specific skills gaps within their workforce and to develop tailored educational programs to bridge these gaps.

Consider a manufacturing company introducing AI-driven predictive maintenance systems. The technical staff might need to learn new programming languages or acquire data analysis skills, while the line managers might need training in interpreting and acting on AI-generated insights. It's essential to understand the nuances of how AI integrates with existing roles and where new competencies are necessary.

Successful upskilling and reskilling initiatives often involve a combination of on-the-job training, online courses, and formal education programs. Companies like IBM and Google have set the benchmark with comprehensive strategies that include partnerships with educational institutions, robust online platforms, and internal mentorship programs. They've shown that creating a diverse educational ecosystem can effectively address the diverse learning needs of employees.

The role of leadership in driving these initiatives is paramount. Encouraging a growth mindset across the organization can break down resistance to change and create a climate where learning is seen as a shared journey rather than a personal hurdle. Forward-thinking leaders champion cultures where experimentation and adaptation are not only supported but celebrated.

Moreover, the impact of these initiatives goes beyond individual benefits. By investing in their workforce, companies cultivate loyalty and reduce turnover. Employees who feel their skills are valued and that they're equipped for future challenges are more likely to exhibit higher job satisfaction and engagement. This, in return, boosts overall organizational performance and resilience in the face of technological disruption.

It's also important to recognize the role of soft skills in the AI-driven workplace. While technical proficiency is crucial, skills such as critical thinking, emotional intelligence, and creativity retain their importance. AI can process data and recognize patterns, but it cannot replace human intuition and empathy—qualities that are essential for leadership and innovation.

Developing these soft skills can be integrated into reskilling programs through interactive workshops, cross-departmental projects, and initiatives that encourage collaboration and problem-solving. The aim is to holistically prepare the workforce for a future where they work alongside AI, using it as a tool to enhance rather than replace their capabilities.

Engaging external partners can provide fresh perspectives and state-of-the-art solutions that internal teams might not have. Collaborations with tech companies and educational institutions can provide access to cutting-edge technologies and knowledge, which are otherwise unavailable internally. This not only accelerates learning but also aligns the organization with the broader trends in technology and workforce development.

It's important to remember that upskilling and reskilling are not finite processes. The rapidly changing technological landscape demands a perpetual commitment to learning. Organizations must continuously revise their training programs to incorporate the latest developments and ensure their workforce remains competitive.

In conclusion, the successful integration of AI into the workplace hinges on a strategic approach to upskilling and reskilling. By fostering an educational culture, leveraging diverse learning methods, and emphasizing both technical and soft skills, businesses can navigate the challenges of AI transformation and ultimately achieve a dynamic and future-ready workforce.

Conclusion

The journey through this book, designed for business leaders and managers, unveils the profound impact of Artificial Intelligence (AI) on strategic decision-making and competitive advantage. With AI rapidly transforming business landscapes, understanding and leveraging its potential has never been more crucial. As we conclude, it's important to reiterate the dynamism and endless possibilities AI brings to the table.

AI is reshaping industries by driving innovation and enabling unprecedented efficiencies. Business decisions are no longer anchored solely in intuition or experience. Instead, they are augmented with data-driven insights and precise predictive capabilities. For leaders, the task is no longer just to understand AI but to champion its integration across departments and processes, fostering a culture that embraces continuous learning and adaptation.

One of the key takeaways from this journey is the pressing need for a solid AI strategy. Such a strategy demands alignment with overarching business objectives, ensuring that AI initiatives directly contribute to organizational goals. This alignment is critical—it prevents resource wastage and guarantees that AI efforts produce tangible value. Moreover, selecting the right AI tools tailored to specific business needs can enhance this alignment, paving the way for successful implementation and added competitive edge.

Ethical considerations also stand out as paramount. AI systems hold enormous potential but carry risks related to bias, privacy, and security. Ensuring that AI deployments respect ethical boundaries is not just a legal requirement but a moral imperative. Establishing trust through transparency and explainability forms the backbone of long-term AI success, influencing both public perception and employee morale.

Adoption challenges persist, from resource constraints to resistance to change. Yet, these challenges offer opportunities for growth and innovation. Leaders equipped with the right mindset embrace these barriers as stepping stones, guiding their teams through cultural shifts and technological advancements. By fostering a data-driven culture, they nurture an environment where AI isn't just a tool but a core component of strategic evolution.

The future of AI isn't solely about technological advancements. It's about building a workforce equipped to thrive alongside these innovations. Upskilling and reskilling initiatives are pivotal in preparing employees for a future where AI and human intelligence coalesce, driving superior outcomes. Empowering employees to harness AI capabilities ensures a dynamic and responsive workforce ready for tomorrow's challenges.

In examining AI's impact across industries, from healthcare to retail, the common thread is AI's ability to revolutionize the customer experience. Whether through personalized marketing, optimized supply chains, or enhanced customer support, AI's potential to redefine interaction points is immense. As firms aim for market dominance, leveraging AI to anticipate customer needs and streamline processes becomes a game-changer.

Looking forward, the emphasis on regulatory compliance will intensify. Navigating complex legal landscapes and understanding regional differences ensures that AI systems remain compliant and ethically sound. As regulations evolve, so too will the frameworks businesses use to evaluate and deploy AI technologies, necessitating a forward-thinking and adaptable approach.

In conclusion, the AI landscape is vast and continually evolving. For those willing to innovate and lead with AI, the future promises incredible opportunities. The blueprint is clear: develop strategic AI alignment, prioritize ethical standards, overcome adoption challenges, and build a competent, AI-literate workforce. By doing so, businesses not only remain competitive but become frontrunners in their industries.

As you venture beyond this book, let your approach to AI be bold yet informed, visionary yet grounded in ethics. Embrace AI not as a future distant possibility but as a current critical asset. Armed with insights from this journey, you're now equipped to harness AI not only to adapt but to thrive, setting new benchmarks in strategic business leadership.

Appendix A:
Appendix

In the dynamic landscape of business, the confluence of data and AI technologies is creating unprecedented opportunities for growth and transformation. With the preceding chapters exploring the multifaceted applications of AI across sectors, this appendix aims to provide additional insights that can be instrumental in navigating the AI revolution effectively. While the core content of this book has delved into the principles, strategies, and challenges of AI integration, this section serves as a supplementary guide, offering practical tips, resources, and reflections that reinforce the overarching themes presented earlier.

To fully harness the potential of AI, it's crucial to remain adaptable and continuously evolve your approach. Learning from both successes and setbacks is a part of this journey. Here, we've compiled key considerations for business leaders to keep in mind:

- **Continuous Learning:** The AI landscape is ever-evolving. It's important to foster an environment of continuous education and curiosity within your teams. Encourage your workforce to engage with the latest developments and take advantage of learning platforms and resources that enhance AI understanding.

- **Collaboration:** AI is a field that thrives on collaboration. By fostering partnerships and networks within and beyond your organization, you can tap into a wealth of diverse insights and experiences that can drive innovation and reduce redundancy.

- **Adaptive Mindset:** Be prepared to pivot strategies as new information and technologies emerge. Flexibility is essential for responding to both the challenges and opportunities AI presents.

- **Ethics and Responsibility:** As addressed in the ethical considerations chapter, maintaining ethical standards is vital. Always prioritize transparency, fairness, and accountability in AI implementations to help build trust with stakeholders.

- **Resource Allocation:** Effective resource allocation is a cornerstone of successful AI projects. Ensure your teams have access to the necessary tools, talent, and infrastructure to incorporate AI initiatives seamlessly into business operations.

The information and strategies outlined in this appendix aim to equip you with a grounded perspective for navigating the continuing evolution of AI in business. As you move forward, remember that AI is more than just a tool—it's a catalyst for change that, when wielded thoughtfully, can lead to groundbreaking advancements. Embrace the journey with a spirit of exploration and an unwavering commitment to shaping a future where technology and humanity flourish together.

The transformative power of AI is only beginning to be realized, and your role as a leader is pivotal in guiding your organization through this transformative era. Stay curious, stay informed, and most importantly, be ready to lead the change.

www.ingramcontent.com/pod-product-compliance
Lightning Source LLC
Chambersburg PA
CBHW032009170526
45157CB00002B/620